THE FOUNDATIONS
OF EMPIRICAL KNOWLEDGE

THE FOUNDATIONS

OF

EMPIRICAL KNOWLEDGE

BY

ALFRED J. AYER, M.A., F.B.A.

FELLOW OF NEW COLLEGE AND
WYKEHAM PROFESSOR OF LOGIC IN THE UNIVERSITY
OF OXFORD

WITHDRAWN

LONDON

MACMILLAN & CO LTD

NEW YORK · ST MARTIN'S PRESS

1962

—

First Edition 1940
Reprinted 1947, 1951, 1953, 1955, 1958, 1962

MACMILLAN AND COMPANY LIMITED
St Martin's Street London WC 2
also Bombay Calcutta Madras Melbourne

THE MACMILLAN COMPANY OF CANADA LIMITED
Toronto

ST MARTIN'S PRESS INC
New York

PRINTED IN GREAT BRITAIN

TO
VALERIE AYER

PREFACE

THE title of this book covers a wide range of subjects ; and I do not wish to claim that I have investigated them all. My main purpose has been to resolve the philosophical problems which are commonly brought under the heading of " our knowledge of the external world ". But I have also found occasion to deal with such further questions as those of our knowledge of other minds, of the character of causal laws, of the analysis of meaning, and of the nature of propositions and their relation to facts.

Where I believe that I am indebted to other authors I have made my acknowledgements in the text. But I should like here to pay a tribute to Professor H. H. Price's work on *Perception*, to which I owe considerably more than my frequent criticisms of it would suggest.

My thanks are due also to my friend Mr. C. E. Stevens for reading the proofs.

A. J. AYER

BRIGADE OF GUARDS DEPÔT,
CATERHAM, SURREY,
March, 1940

CONTENTS

ix

I

THE ARGUMENT FROM ILLUSION

1. Exposition of the Argument

It does not normally occur to us that there is any need for us to justify our belief in the existence of material things. At the present moment, for example, I have no doubt whatsoever that I really am perceiving the familiar objects, the chairs and table, the pictures and books and flowers with which my room is furnished ; and I am therefore satisfied that they exist. I recognize indeed that people are sometimes deceived by their senses, but this does not lead me to suspect that my own sense-perceptions cannot in general be trusted, or even that they may be deceiving me now. And this is not, I believe, an exceptional attitude. I believe that, in practice, most people agree with John Locke that " the certainty of things existing *in rerum natura*, when we have the testimony of our senses for it, is not only as great as our frame can attain to, but as our condition needs." [1]

When, however, one turns to the writings of those philosophers who have recently concerned

---

[1] *An Essay concerning Human Understanding*, Book IV, ch. 2, section viii.

themselves with the subject of perception, one may begin to wonder whether this matter is quite so simple. It is true that they do, in general, allow that our belief in the existence of material things is well founded ; some of them, indeed, would say that there were occasions on which we knew for certain the truth of such propositions as " this is a cigarette " or " this is a pen ". But even so they are not, for the most part, prepared to admit that such objects as pens or cigarettes are ever directly perceived. What, in their opinion, we directly perceive is always an object of a different kind from these ; one to which it is now customary to give the name of " sense-datum ". These sense-data are said to have the " presentative function " [1] of making us conscious of material things. But how they perform this function, and what is their relation to the material things which they present, are questions about which there is much dispute. There is dispute also about the properties of sense-data, apart from their relationship to material things : whether, for example, they are each of them private to a single observer ; whether they can appear to have qualities that they do not really have, or have qualities that they do not appear to have ; whether they are in any sense " within " the percipient's mind or brain. I shall show later on that these are not empirical questions. They are to be settled by making it clear how the term " sense-datum " is intended to be used. But first I must explain why it is thought necessary to

[1] Cf. H. H. Price, *Perception*, p. 104.

introduce such a term at all. Why may we not say
that we are directly aware of material things ?

The answer is provided by what is known as the
argument from illusion. This argument, as it is
ordinarily stated, is based on the fact that material
things may present different appearances to different
observers, or to the same observer in different conditions, and that the character of these appearances
is to some extent causally determined by the state
of the conditions and the observer. For instance,
it is remarked that a coin which looks circular from
one point of view may look elliptical from another ;
or that a stick which normally appears straight looks
bent when it is seen in water ; or that to people who
take drugs such as mescal, things appear to change
their colours. The familiar cases of mirror images,
and double vision, and complete hallucinations, such
as the mirage, provide further examples. Nor is
this a peculiarity of visual appearances. The same
thing occurs in the domains of the other senses,
including the sense of touch. It may be pointed
out, for example, that the taste that a thing appears
to have may vary with the condition of the palate ;
or that a liquid will seem to have a different temperature according as the hand that is feeling it is itself
hot or cold ; or that a coin seems larger when it is
placed on the tongue than when it is held in the palm
of the hand ; or, to take a case of complete hallucination, that people who have had limbs amputated may
still continue to feel pain in them.

Let us now consider one of these examples, say

that of the stick which is refracted in water, and see what is to be inferred. For the present it must be assumed that the stick does not really change its shape when it is placed in water. I shall discuss the meaning and validity of this assumption later on. Then it follows that at least one of the visual appearances of the stick is delusive ; for it cannot be both crooked and straight. Nevertheless, even in the case where what we see is not the real quality of a material thing, it is supposed that we are still seeing something; and that it is convenient to give this a name. And it is for this purpose that philosophers have recourse to the term " sense-datum ". By using it they are able to give what seems to them a satisfactory answer to the question: What is the object of which we are directly aware, in perception, if it is not part of any material thing ? Thus, when a man sees a mirage in the desert, he is not thereby perceiving any material thing; for the oasis which he thinks he is perceiving does not exist. At the same time, it is argued, his experience is not an experience of nothing ; it has a definite content. Accordingly, it is said that he is experiencing sense-data, which are similar in character to what he would be experiencing if he were seeing a real oasis, but are delusive in the sense that the material thing which they appear to present is not actually there. Or again, when I look at myself in the glass my body appears to be some distance behind the glass ; but other observations indicate that it is in front of it. Since it is impossible for my body to be in both these places at once, these perceptions cannot all be veridical. I believe, in fact, that the ones that are delusive are those in which my body appears to be behind the glass. But can it be denied that when one looks at oneself in the glass one is seeing something ? And if, in this case, there really is no such material thing as my body in the place where it appears to be, what is it that I am seeing ? Once again the answer we are invited to give is that it is a sense-datum. And the same conclusion may be reached by taking any other of my examples.

If anything is established by this, it can be only that there are some cases in which the character of our perceptions makes it necessary for us to say that what we are directly experiencing is not a material thing but a sense-datum. It has not been shown that this is so in all cases. It has not been denied, but rather assumed, that there are some perceptions that do present material things to us as they really are ; and in their case there seems at first sight to be no ground for saying that we directly experience sense-data rather than material things. But, as I have already remarked, there is general agreement among the philosophers who make use of the term " sense-datum ", or some equivalent term, that what we immediately experience is always a sense-datum and never a material thing. And for this they give further arguments which I shall now examine.

In the first place it is pointed out that there is no intrinsic difference in kind between those of our perceptions that are veridical in their presentation of material things and those that are delusive.[1] When I look at a straight stick, which is refracted in water and so appears crooked, my experience is qualitatively the same as if I were looking at a stick that really was crooked. When, as the result of my putting on green spectacles, the white walls of my room appear to me to be green, my experience is qualitatively the same as if I were perceiving walls that really were green. When people whose legs have been amputated continue to feel pressure upon them, their experience is qualitatively the same as if pressure really were being exerted upon their legs. But, it is argued, if, when our perceptions were delusive, we were always perceiving something of a different kind from what we perceived when they were veridical, we should expect our experience to be qualitatively different in the two cases. We should expect to be able to tell from the intrinsic character of a perception whether it was a perception of a sense-datum or of a material thing. But this is not possible, as the examples that I have given have shown. In some cases there is indeed a distinction with respect to the beliefs to which the experiences give rise, as can be illustrated by my original example. For when, in normal conditions, we have the experience of seeing a straight stick, we believe that there really is a straight stick there ; but when the stick appears crooked, through being refracted in water, we do not believe that it really is crooked ; we do not regard the fact that it looks crooked in

[1] Cf. H. H. Price, *Perception*, p. 31.

water as evidence against its being really straight. It must, however, be remarked that this difference in the beliefs which accompany our perceptions is not grounded in the nature of the perceptions themselves, but depends upon our past experience. We do not believe that the stick which appears crooked when it stands in water really is crooked because we know from past experience that in normal conditions it looks straight. But a child who had not learned that refraction was a means of distortion would naturally believe that the stick really was crooked as he saw it. The fact, therefore, that there is this distinction between the beliefs that accompany veridical and delusive perceptions does not justify the view that these are perceptions of generically different objects, especially as the distinction by no means applies to all cases. For it sometimes happens that a delusive experience is not only qualitatively indistinguishable from one that is veridical but is also itself believed to be veridical, as in the example of the mirage ; and, conversely, there are cases in which experiences that are actually veridical are believed to be delusive, as when we see something so strange or unexpected that we say to ourselves that we must be dreaming. The fact is that from the character of a perception considered by itself, that is, apart from its relation to further sense-experience, it is not possible to tell whether it is veridical or delusive. But whether we are entitled to infer from this that what we immediately experience is always a sense-datum remains still to be seen.

Another fact which is supposed to show that even in the case of veridical perceptions we are not directly aware of material things is that veridical and delusive perceptions may form a continuous series, both with respect to their qualities and with respect to the conditions in which they are obtained.[1] Thus, if I gradually approach an object from a distance I may begin by having a series of perceptions which are delusive in the sense that the object appears to be smaller than it really is. Let us assume that this series terminates in a veridical perception. Then the difference in quality between this perception and its immediate predecessor will be of the same order as the difference between any two delusive perceptions that are next to one another in the series ; and, on the assumption that I am walking at a uniform pace, the same will be true of the difference in the conditions on which the generation of the series depends. A similar example would be that of the continuous alteration in the apparent colour of an object which was seen in a gradually changing light. Here again the relation between a veridical perception and the delusive perception that comes next to it in the series is the same as that which obtains between neighbouring delusive perceptions, both with respect to the difference in quality and with respect to the change in the conditions ; and these are differences of degree and not of kind. But this, it is argued, is not what we should expect if the veridical perception were a perception of an object

[1] Cf. Price, *op. cit.* p. 32.

of a different sort, a material thing as opposed to a ✗
sense-datum.   Does not the fact that veridical and ✗
delusive perceptions shade into one another in the
way that is indicated by these examples show that
the objects that are perceived in either case are
generically the same ?   And from this it would
follow, if it was acknowledged that the delusive perceptions were perceptions of sense-data, that what
we directly experienced was always a sense-datum
and never a material thing.

The final argument that has to be considered in
this context is based upon the fact that all our perceptions, whether veridical or delusive, are to some
extent causally dependent both upon external conditions, such as the character of the light, and upon
our own physiological and psychological states.   In
the case of perceptions that we take to be delusive
this is a fact that we habitually recognize.   We say,
for example, that the stick looks crooked because it
is seen in water ; that the white walls appear green
to me because I am wearing green spectacles ; that
the water feels cool because my hand is hot ; that
the murderer sees the ghost of his victim because of
his bad conscience or because he has been taking
drugs.   In the case of perceptions that we take to
be veridical we are apt not to notice such causal
dependencies, since as a rule it is only the occurrence
of the unexpected or the abnormal that induces us
to look for a cause.   But in this matter also there is
no essential difference between veridical and delusive
perceptions.   When, for example, I look at the piece

of paper on which I am writing, I may claim that I am seeing it as it really is. But I must admit that in order that I should have this experience it is not sufficient that there should actually be such a piece of paper there. Many other factors are necessary, such as the condition of the light, the distance at which I am from the paper, the nature of the background, the state of my nervous system and my eyes. A proof that they are necessary is that if I vary them I find that I have altered the character of my perception. Thus, if I screw up my eyes I see two pieces of paper instead of one ; if I grow dizzy the appearance of the paper becomes blurred ; if I alter my position sufficiently it appears to have a different shape and size ; if the light is extinguished, or another object is interposed, I cease to see it altogether. On the other hand, the converse does not hold. If the paper is removed I shall cease to see it ; but the state of the light or of my nervous system or any other of the factors that were relevant to the occurrence of my perception may still remain the same. From this it may be inferred that the relation between my perception and these accompanying conditions is such that, while they are not causally dependent upon it, it is causally dependent upon them. And the same would apply to any other instance of a veridical perception that one cared to choose.

This point being established, the argument proceeds as follows. It is held to be characteristic of material things that their existence and their essential properties are independent of any particular observer.

For they are supposed to continue the same, whether they are observed by one person or another, or not observed at all. But this, it is argued, has been shown not to be true of the objects we immediately experience. And so the conclusion is reached that what we immediately experience is in no case a material thing. According to this way of reasoning, if some perceptions are rightly held to be veridical, and others delusive, it is because of the different relations in which their objects stand to material things, and it is a philosophical problem to discover what these relations are. We may be allowed to have indirect knowledge of the properties of material things. But this knowledge, it is held, must be obtained through the medium of sense-data, since they are the only objects of which, in sense-perception, we are immediately aware.

2. Evaluation of the Argument from Illusion

With this I complete my exposition of the so-called argument from illusion. In considering its validity it is important first to determine whether the question it raises concerning the nature of the objects that we directly perceive is to be regarded as a question of language or as a question of fact. In most cases the philosophers who have made use of this argument have taken it to prove a matter of fact. They have inferred from it, not merely that it is linguistically inconvenient, but that it is false to say that we are ever directly aware of a material thing. But if the argument is interpreted in this way it is evidently not conclusive. In the first place, when one examines the subsidiary arguments which are supposed to prove that what we perceive when our perceptions are veridical cannot be generically different from what we perceive when they are delusive, one finds that each of them rests upon a premise that is open to question. It is taken for granted that if veridical and delusive perceptions were perceptions of objects of different types, they would always be qualitatively distinguishable ; or that they would not, in respect of their qualities and the conditions of their occurrence, be capable of being ranged in a continuous series ; or thirdly, that material things can exist and have properties without being causally dependent on any observer. But each of these assumptions could be denied without self-contradiction. Nor do the first two appear to admit of any empirical proof. As for the third, it is true that we find reason to believe a number of hypo-thetical propositions about the experiences that we should be having if we were in certain situations in which we actually are not. And if the proposition that material things are causally independent of our observation of them is understood to imply no more than that some such hypothetical propositions are true even though their protases are never fulfilled, we may consider ourselves justified in maintaining it on inductive grounds. But though this is perhaps the most natural way to interpret this proposition, and the one that I shall adopt myself, it is not the interpretation that is required by the argument from illusion. For these hypothetical propositions concerning what we should observe in certain unfulfilled conditions might very well be true of objects whose manifestations proved, when we actually did observe them, to be causally dependent upon our observation. If, therefore, the proposition that material things are independent of our observation of them means no more than the certain hypothetical propositions about our sense-experiences may be both true and unfulfilled, it does not entail the conclusion that the objects we directly perceive, being causally dependent upon the state of the observer and the accompanying conditions, are not material things. But if we have to interpret the proposition in such a way that it does entail this conclusion, then it no longer appears capable of being justified on empirical grounds. It might indeed be made a matter of definition that material things should be causally independent of any process of observation, in some sense from which it would follow, in conjunction with the facts I have mentioned about the causes of our sense-experiences, that the objects of which we were immediately aware could not be material things. But the consequence of this would be that such objects as pens and books and tables, as they are ordinarily conceived, could not in virtue of this definition any longer be counted as material things. And it was with objects such as these that the argument which the definition is supposed to save was primarily concerned.

So far I have been maintaining only that the argument from illusion does not prove that we are always mistaken in believing that the objects we directly perceive are material things, if the question What kind of objects do we directly perceive ? is taken as a question of fact. But does the argument prove even that there are *any* cases of perception in which such a belief would be mistaken ? I have shown that the ground on which it is maintained that there are at any rate some occasions on which we perceive sense-data which are not parts of any material things is that some perceptions are delusive ; and the ground on which it is maintained that some of our perceptions must be delusive is that if we take them all to be veridical we shall involve ourselves in contradictions, since we shall have to attribute to material things such mutually incompatible pro-perties as being at the same time both green and yellow, or both elliptical and round. But here it may be objected that these contradictions cannot, in fact, be derived from the nature of our perceptions alone. If from one standpoint I see what appears to be a round coin and then, subsequently, from another standpoint, see it as elliptical, there is no contradiction involved in my supposing that in each case I am seeing the coin as it really is. This sup-position becomes self-contradictory only when it is combined with the assumption that the real shape of the coin has remained the same. Similarly, if someone whom I call colour-blind sees as red what I see as green, the proposition that our perceptions

are both veridical is not contradictory in itself. The
contradiction arises only when one adds the assumption that we are both seeing the same material thing.
Nor again, in the case where one puts both one's
hands simultaneously into a vessel of water and finds
that it seems cold to one hand and hot to the other,
is it self-contradictory to hold that both these
experiences are veridical. To obtain the contradiction it must also be assumed that the temperature
of the water with which the vessel is filled is really
the same throughout. And so it goes with all the
examples, including those in which the experience
of one sense is supposed to contradict that of another,
and those in which our perceptions are held to be
completely hallucinatory. For instance, if a stick
that looks crooked at the same time feels straight,
it is not logically impossible that both these perceptions should be veridical. It becomes so only if one
makes suitable assumptions about the correlation of
the domains of sight and touch. And in the case
of the mirage, it is only if we make suitable assumptions about the duration of material things and their
accessibility to different observers that we are obliged
to hold that the trees and the water which the observer
in question thinks he is perceiving do not really
exist.

But now let us suppose that instead of recognizing
these alleged contradictions and attempting to evade
them by saying that we immediately experience
sense-data which are not parts of material things,
we choose rather to deny the supplementary assump-

tions which are required for the contradictions to result. None of these assumptions is logically necessary, so that if they are to be validated it must be on empirical grounds. What then is the nature of the empirical evidence upon which they rest? The answer is that it is in every instance a matter of our being able to establish a certain order among our experiences. We say that an object seen in a looking-glass is not really in the place in which it appears to be, because, when we go to that place, we find that there is no such object there to be seen or touched. We say that a penny which appears to have a different shape when it is seen from a different angle has not really changed its shape, because, when we return to our original point of view, we find that it looks the same shape as it did before. We say that a man who sees as red what we see as green is nevertheless seeing the same object as ourselves, because of the observations that we make concerning his behaviour; for example, we may have the experience of hearing him describe it, apart from its colour, in the same way as we should ourselves, or if we ask him to touch it we may see what appears to be his finger coinciding with an appearance of the object in our own visual fields. We say that the temperature of the water that feels hot to one hand and cold to the other is really uniform, because it is observed to yield a uniform reading on a thermometer. We say, in the instance of the mirage, that the trees do not really exist, because we believe that people who were in what we should call a normal physiological state would

not perceive them and because they cannot subsequently be perceived by the observer himself.

Now, having described the nature of the evidence
that is ordinarily thought to be sufficient to establish
these various assumptions, I wish to consider what
would be the position of one who, though he acknowledged the particular facts about our experiences that
constitute this evidence, still chose to deny the propositions about material things that these facts are
supposed to prove. One may imagine his saying, for
example, that the fact that the shape of the penny
still appears the same when the observer returns to
his original point of view does not prove that its real
shape has been unchanged ; for it might be the case
that the shape that it originally appeared to have was
in reality altered and then regained. Or again, he
might say that the fact that I observe another person
behaving in the way I should expect him to behave
if he were seeing the same object as I am myself
does not prove that he really is seeing the same object ;
it may show that the structure of his world is in a
large measure similar to that of my own, but it does
not follow that its contents are the same. And I
have no doubt that by postulating a greater number
of material things and regarding them as being more
variable and evanescent than we normally do, it
would be possible to deal with all the other cases
in a similar way. How then is one who holds this
position to be refuted ? The answer is that so long
as we persist in regarding the issue as one concerning
a matter of fact it is impossible for us to refute him.

We cannot refute him, because, as far as the facts are concerned, there is really no dispute between us. It has been assumed that he agrees with us about the nature of the sensible appearances ; and no evidence of any other kind is or can be available. In what then does our disagreement consist ? It consists in the fact that he refuses to describe the phenomena in the way in which we describe them. Where we say that the real shape of a coin is unchanging, he prefers to say that its shape is really undergoing some cyclical process of change. Where we say that two observers are seeing the same material thing, he prefers to say that they are seeing different things which have, however, some structural properties in common. But the facts to which these expressions are intended to refer are in either case the same. In other words, we are not disputing about the validity of two conflicting sets of hypotheses, but about the choice of two different languages. The dispute appears to be concerned with a matter of fact because our opponent uses the same form of words as we use ourselves ; but since the empirical evidence which we regard as justifying the employment of these words is not so regarded by him, it is to be inferred that he is assigning to the words a different meaning from that which we have given them. Assuming that his language is self-consistent, we may still criticize it on the ground that it is cumbersome and incon-venient. And we may argue in support of some other terminology, such as the terminology of sense-data, that it involves a less radical departure from normal usage. But at the same time we must recognize that the superiority of the language that we favour, if it is superior, does not consist in the expression of any truth that our opponent disregards or denies. For if there is here to be any question of truth or falsehood, there must be some disagreement about the nature of the empirical facts. And in this case no such disagreement exists.

3. The Introduction of Sense-data

The conclusion that I have now reached is that in order to account for our perceptual experience, it is not necessary to maintain that any of our perceptions are delusive. And in saying this I am not attempting to deny the empirical facts which the proposition that some of our perceptions are delusive is ordinarily understood to express. I am pointing out merely that this is not the only way of describing them. I have argued that these facts do not render it impossible to hold that what is perceived is always a material thing, provided that one makes suitable assumptions about the constitution and behaviour of the material things in question. But since these assumptions are not factual but linguistic in character, the effect of making them is to give to the expression " material thing " a different meaning from that which is ordinarily given to it. I have, therefore, not yet answered the question that I originally set out to discuss. For I have not yet succeeded in showing that it is logically possible both to admit the facts that are ordinarily expressed by saying that some perceptions are delusive, and also to maintain that, in the case of such perceptions, we directly perceive material things, in the ordinary sense. It may be granted that the argument from illusion does not prove that it is necessary, in describing our perceptual experience, to use any word in precisely the same way as philosophers have proposed to use the word " sense-datum ". But does it not prove that we need to make at any rate some alteration in our ordinary way of speaking if we are to be able to describe all the empirical facts ?

I do not think that even this limited claim can be justified. It is indeed true that, if we restrict ourselves to using words in such a way that to say of an object that it is seen or touched or otherwise perceived entails saying that it really exists and that something really has the character that the object appears to have, we shall be obliged either to deny that any perceptions are delusive or else to admit that it is a mistake to speak as if the objects that we perceived were always material things. But the fact is that in our ordinary usage we are not so restricted. Thus, to return to the familiar examples, if I say that I am seeing a stick which looks crooked, I do not imply that anything really is crooked, or if I say that someone is feeling pressure on his leg, I do not necessarily exclude the possibility that his leg has been amputated, or if, being subject to an illusion of double vision, I say that I am perceiving two pieces of paper, I need not be implying that there really are two pieces of paper there. But surely, it may be said, if the two pieces of paper really are perceived they must both exist in some sense, even if not as material things. The answer to this objection is that it is based on a misunderstanding of the way in which I am using the word " perceive ". I am using it here in such a way that to say of an object that it is perceived does not entail saying that it exists in any sense at all. And this is a perfectly correct and familiar usage of the word.

If there is thought to be a difficulty here, it is perhaps because there is also a correct and familiar usage of the word " perceive ", in which to say of an object that it is perceived does carry the implication that it exists. If I decide to use the word " perceive " in this sense, I cannot then describe my illusion of double vision by saying " I perceived two pieces of paper but there was really only one piece there ". Instead I may say " I thought I perceived two pieces of paper but I was really perceiving only one ". At this point someone may be tempted to ask " Which was it that you really perceived ? Two pieces of paper or one ? " and to imagine that he is raising a question of fact. But this would be a mistake. For the fact which I am purporting to describe is the same, whichever method of description I choose. Assuming that the proposition which I am intending to express is true, all that is needed to settle the question whether I did or did not really perceive two pieces of paper is that we should decide what we mean by " perceiving ". If the word is used in one familiar sense, it can be said that I really did perceive two pieces of paper. If it is used in another sense, which is also sanctioned by convention, then it must be said that I perceived only one. In the sense of " perceiving " in which it is impossible to perceive what does not exist the word is not applicable to experiences that are existentially delusive. In this sense I did not perceive two pieces of paper ; I only thought that I perceived them. What I really perceived was one piece of paper, if only one piece existed ; or if it be assumed that my experience was totally hallucinatory, I did not really perceive anything at all. I was indeed having an experience that could properly be described as perceptual in one sense of the word. But in this sense there is no objection to my saying that I really did perceive two pieces of paper, even if they did not both exist. There is no problem so long as one keeps the two usages distinct.

The same ambiguity is to be found in the way in which we describe perceptions that are qualitatively delusive. For example, a man will say that he sees a distant star which has an extension greater than that of the earth ; but if he is asked to describe what it is that he is actually seeing, he may say that it is a silvery speck no bigger than a sixpence. Now, since it is impossible that the star should both be bigger than the earth and at the same time no bigger than a sixpence, one is tempted to conclude that one at least of these assertions is false. And, in fact, many philosophers would say that the man was mistaken

in asserting that he saw the star. But this is to
ignore the fact that the word " see ", like the word
" perceive ", is commonly used in a variety of senses.
In one sense, the sense in which the man can say
truly that he sees the star, it is necessary that what
is seen should really exist, but not necessary that it
should have the qualities that it appears to have. In
another sense, which is that in which the man can
say truly that what he sees is no bigger than a sixpence, it is not possible that anything should seem
to have qualities that it does not really have, but
also not necessary that what is seen should really
exist. If, in our example, it is assumed that the man
is using the word " see " consistently, then it does
follow that at least one of his statements is empirically
false. But it is also open to us to accept both his
statements if we assume, as indeed we ordinarily
should, that he has slipped from one to the other
usage of the word " see ". The important point to
notice is that we do not require the two usages in
order to describe the facts. Let us suppose that, in
our example, the man decides to use the word " see "
only in the sense in which he is justified in saying
that he sees the star. How, then, is he to express the
fact that what he sees in the other sense is a speck
no bigger than a sixpence ? Simply by using the
phrase " appears to be " instead of " is ". And this
terminology of " appearing " is one that we do very
often use in describing facts of this sort. That we
are accustomed also to describe them in another
way, which involves a different usage of words like

" see " and " perceive ", is not ordinarily a source of confusion to us, because we are able to tell from the context what is the sense in which such words are intended to be understood. But it has misled philosophers, as their use of the argument from illusion shows.

In order to avoid these ambiguities, what the advocates of the sense-datum theory have done is to decide both to apply the word " see " or any other words that designate modes of perception to delusive as well as to veridical experiences, and at the same time to use these words in such a way that what is seen or otherwise sensibly experienced must really exist and must really have the properties that it appears to have. No doubt they also use these words in other, more familiar, senses. But it is this usage that leads them to the introduction of sense-data. For, having adopted it, they find that they cannot then say, in the case of a delusive perception, that what is experienced is a material thing ; for either the requisite material thing does not exist, or else it has not got the requisite property. And so they say that it is a sense-datum. And instead of saying that this sense-datum is perceived, they say that it is sensed. But if in the case of a delusive perception one is going to say that one is sensing a sense-datum, then, inasmuch as the distinction between delusive and veridical perceptions is not a distinction of quality, it is convenient to extend this usage to all cases. That is to say, the contention that if these perceptions are not qualitatively distinguishable the objects perceived must be of the same type, which I saw no reason for accepting when it was treated as a statement of fact, can reasonably be accepted as a rule of language. And thus one arrives at the conclusion that in all cases of perception the objects of which one is directly aware are sense-data and not material things.

This procedure is in itself legitimate ; and for certain purposes it is useful. I shall indeed adopt it myself. But one must not suppose that it embodies any factual discovery. The philosopher who says that he is seeing a sense-datum in a case where most people would say that they were seeing a material thing is not contradicting the received opinion on any question of fact. He is not putting forward a new hypothesis which could be empirically verified or confuted. What he is doing is simply to recommend a new verbal usage.[1] He is proposing to us that instead of speaking, for example, of seeing a straight stick which looks crooked, or of seeing an oasis when there is no oasis there, we should speak of seeing a sense-datum which really has the quality of being crooked, and which belongs to a straight stick, or of seeing a sense-datum which really has the qualities that are characteristic of the appearance of an oasis, but does not belong to any material thing. If we accept this recommendation it will not be because our ordinary language is defective, in the sense that it does not furnish us with the means of

[1] This point has been clearly brought out by G. A. Paul in his paper on " Is there a Problem about Sense-data ? ", *Aristotelian Society Supplementary Proceedings*, 1936.

describing all the facts, or in the sense that it obliges us to misdescribe some of them; but simply because it is not so good an instrument as the sense-datum language for our special purposes. For since in philosophizing about perception our main object is to analyse the relationship of our sense-experiences to the propositions we put forward concerning material things, it is useful for us to have a terminology that enables us to refer to the contents of our experiences independently of the material things that they are taken to present. And this the sense-datum language provides.[1] It has also the advantage of laying down an unambiguous convention for the use of words that stand for modes of perception, and so freeing us from the verbal problems that develop, as we have seen, out of the ambiguous use of such words in ordinary speech. We may admit, therefore, that there are good grounds for adopting this technical terminology. But in adopting it we must realize that it does not in itself add to our knowledge of empirical facts, or even make it possible for us to express anything that we could not have expressed without it. At the best it enables us only to refer to familiar facts in a clearer and more convenient way.

The main proposition which the argument from illusion, as I have interpreted it, was supposed to establish was that what we see, or otherwise directly experience, are never material things, but only sense-data. This conclusion I accept, but not as a pro-

---

[1] Not fully, indeed, but to an extent that is sufficient for our purpose. *Vide* Part V of this book.

position in the ordinary sense. A way of making this distinction clear is to contrast the sentence " I never see material things but only sense-data " with some sentence of similar appearance that does express a proposition about a matter of fact. Consider, for example, the sentence " I never see gold sovereigns but only Bank of England notes ". The proposition which this sentence expresses is one whose validity is subject to empirical tests. My present experience confirms it, but at the same time I can imagine having perceptions that would confute it. My experience would be different if it were false. But when I say " I never see material things but only sense-data " I am saying something the truth or falsehood of which makes no difference whatsoever to the nature of my experience. Indeed it is misleading to speak of truth or falsehood at all in this case. For if we allow ourselves to say that the sentence " I never see material things but only sense-data " expresses either a true or a false proposition, we thereby suggest that it is on a level with sentences like " I never see gold sovereigns but only Bank of England notes " ; that its validity depends upon empirical facts. But I have shown that between a philosopher who says that he sees only sense-data and one who says that he sees material things there is no disagreement about any matter of fact. If they appeal to the facts at all it can be only to show that one form of expression is more convenient than the other. Thus, the sense in which my experience gives me justification for saying that I see only sense-data is quite different from the sense in which it gives me justification for saying that I see only Bank of England notes. In the latter case it is a question of the verification of an empirical proposition. In the case of the sense-data it is a question of there being extraneous grounds for preferring one method of description to another, which is equally true to the facts. And this shows that there is a generic difference in the meaning of the two sentences in spite of the similarity of their appearances. In one case we are expressing a proposition about an empirical matter of fact ; in the other case we are expressing a resolution about the usage of words. We may appeal to experience to show that such a resolution is sensible or foolish, but we cannot properly claim that it is either true or false.

4. Misuses of the Argument from Illusion

But is this all that the argument from illusion yields us ; a motive for adopting a new terminology ? It seems a meagre result when one considers how much importance has been attached to the argument by writers on the theory of knowledge. In one form or another it has been used to support such con- clusions as that the world of sensible phenomena is self-contradictory ; that our ideas of secondary qualities are not resemblances of any real qualities of material things ; which means, *inter alia*, that no material thing is literally coloured, or literally charac- terized by any sensible temperature or weight ; that the primary qualities of solidity, extension, number, figure and motion are also " not real " ; that the testimony of the senses is not to be relied on, and that if we have any acquaintance with material things as they really are, it is not through any act of sense-perception but only through some " intuition of the mind ". But all such uses of the argument are invalid, as I shall now proceed to show.

I may begin by pointing out that if the assertion that the world of sensible phenomena is self-contradictory is taken literally, no argument can possibly prove it, for the reason that the notion of self-contradiction is not applicable to the phenomena themselves. It does not make sense to say of different phenomena either that they do or that they do not contradict one another ; they simply occur. It is only with regard to the propositions that we use to describe the phenomena that the question of con-tradiction can legitimately be raised. Let us there-fore assume that what the argument from illusion is supposed to prove is that it is impossible to describe whatever phenomena occur without sooner or later falling into self-contradiction. But so far from proving this, the argument does not show even that any contradiction is involved in the propositions that we actually use to describe phenomena. It shows that we speak of material things as appearing to exist in some conditions and not in others, or to some observers and not to others, and that we speak of them as appearing to have incompatible qualities to different observers, and in different conditions ; but in all this there is no contradiction. It is not self-contradictory to say that a penny that looks round from one standpoint looks elliptical from another, or that a curtain that looks green to me appears to some other person to be blue. It is not self-contradictory to say both that a man feels pain in an amputated leg, and that the leg is not perceptible to any other observer or subsequently to the man himself. And the same would hold good of any other example that could be produced.

But this, I may be told, is only because I am treating the appearances as mere appearances. Treat them as realities ; assume that things really have the qualities that they appear to have, and contradictions arise at once. As Bradley says, " a thing must be self-consistent and self-dependent. It either has a quality or has not got it. And if it has it, it cannot have it only sometimes, and merely in this or that relation. But such a principle is the condemnation of secondary qualities ",[1] and, as he later adds, of primary qualities also.

If this argument is intended to apply not merely to the language that we actually use but also to any alternative language in which we might attempt to describe the same facts, then I have already refuted it. For I have shown that a language in which no distinction is made between things as they appear and things as they really are need not be self-contradictory. In such a language, a statement that a material thing, M, appeared to have a quality, a,

[1] *Appearance and Reality*, pp. 11-12.

would always entail that M really did have α, but this would not lead to contradictions, provided that the language also contained suitable criteria, which would, of course, be different from the criteria that we now employ, for determining when a thing changed its qualities and when two appearances were appearances of the same thing. It is true, indeed, that if we abolished the distinction that we ordinarily make between appearance and reality, and at the same time refused to introduce any compensatory conventions, we should be involved in self-contradiction. But why should one be expected to do this ? The argument which I am considering does not furnish any reason.

Furthermore, is it true even that we do avoid contradictions only by treating all appearances as mere appearances ? Admittedly, we do not speak as if every perception were veridical. We use such sentences as " The curtains look green in this light, but they are really blue " ; " The penny looks elliptical from this angle, but it is really round ". But this does not mean that we speak as if every perception were delusive. We assume, in fact, that some of our perceptions are veridical and others not. And in this there is no contradiction. There would be a contradiction only if the same appearances were held to be both veridical and delusive in the same sense ; and this is not the case. What we actually do is to define the real qualities of a material thing in terms of the qualities of certain privileged appearances. Later on it will be shown that this is not an arbitrary procedure ; that an appearance is held to be privileged, in this sense, because of certain special relations that it bears to other appearances, a proposition which will be stated more clearly in the terminology of sense-data.[1] But even if the procedure were arbitrary, which it is not, there would still be no ground for saying that it led to any contradictions. There is no logical reason why, in classifying appearances as veridical or delusive, we should have to include them all in the same category.

A more moderate and common use of the argument from illusion is that in which it is taken to show, not that the assumption that certain sensible qualities literally characterize material things involves any contradiction, but that it is always false. For this, recourse is had to what Professor Price has called the causal form of the argument,[2] with which I have already dealt in a slightly different context.[3] It is pointed out that the appearance of these sensible qualities to an observer depends, as I have shown, upon other factors than the state of the material thing which he supposes them to characterize, among these factors being the physiological and psychological condition of the observer himself. And from this it is inferred that the sensible qualities do not really characterize the material thing in question, or at least that no one has any ground for believing that they do. To quote Bradley again, " A thing is coloured, but not coloured in the same way to every eye ; and except to some eye, it seems not coloured

---

[1] *Vide* Part V, Section 24, of this book.
[2] *Perception*, pp. 27 ff. [3] P. 9.

at all. Is it then coloured or not? And the eye—relation to which appears somehow to make the quality — does that itself possess colour? Clearly not so, unless there is another eye which sees it. Nothing therefore is really coloured ; colour seems only to belong to what itself is colourless. And the same result holds again, with cold and heat. A thing may be cold or hot according to different parts of my skin ; and without some relation to a skin, it seems without any such quality. And, by a like argument, the skin is proved not itself to own the quality, which is hence possessed by nothing. . . . The argument shows everywhere that things have secondary qualities only for an organ ; and that the organ itself has these qualities in no other way." [1]

This is, substantially, a recapitulation of the argument by which Locke sought to prove that ideas of secondary qualities were not resemblances of any real qualities of material things ; and it has been a source of surprise to subsequent philosophers that he did not extend this conclusion to the ideas of primary qualities also. For they have pointed out that it is equally true of the sensible qualities of solidity, extension, figure, number and motion that " things have them only for an organ, and that the organ itself has them in no other way ". This criticism is justified ; but we must not therefore infer that the distinction which Locke drew between primary and secondary qualities [2] is altogether arbitrary. For it

[1] *Op. cit.* p. 12.
[2] Vide *An Essay concerning Human Understanding*, Book II, ch. 8 and ch. 23.

is possible to account for it, if we regard it as forming part of a causal theory of perception. The underlying assumption is that we are entitled to ascribe to material things only those qualities that are necessary and sufficient to cause a given observer to have the sensations that he does ; and these, it is held, are the so-called primary qualities. Thus, the view that the quality of colour does not literally characterize any material thing was maintained, I suggest, not merely because of the argument from illusion, but also because it was thought that sensations of colour could be sufficiently accounted for in terms of the motion of particles which had, besides motion, the primary qualities of solidity, number, figure and extension, but were themselves colourless.[1] It is, however, to be remarked that even if this was a valid line of argument it would not prove that material things were not literally coloured, but only that we had no good reason to suppose that they were ; nor would it prove, what Locke appears to have held, that particular ideas of primary qualities were ever exact resemblances of the real qualities of any given material thing, but only that material things were characterized by some particular qualities of the primary kind. It would entitle us to infer, for example, that a material thing had some quality of extension, but not that it had precisely that quality of which, to use Locke's terminology, we received

---

[1] Another, and perhaps the fundamental, source of the distinction between primary and secondary qualities is the identification of what is real with what is quantitatively measurable. I refer to this point in the last section of this book.

on any particular occasion a simple idea. It is, however, unnecessary to elaborate this point, because the argument is in fact invalid. For it will be shown later on [1] that the causal theory which it presupposes is itself untenable.

But let us return to the argument which has been supposed by Bradley and others to be " the condemnation of secondary qualities ". The assumption upon which it rests is that if the fact that a thing appears to have a certain quality is causally dependent upon the nature of the environment and the observer, it follows that there is no ground for believing that the thing really has that quality. But if I am right in supposing that the real qualities of a material thing are to be defined in terms of the qualities of some of its appearances, the thing itself indeed being nothing apart from its actual and possible appearances,[2] then this assumption is fallacious. For the question how the appearances come to be manifested does not arise in this context. Let it be granted that the relevant appearances would not, in fact, be met with, unless certain further conditions were fulfilled ; there is still no inconsistency in taking their qualities to be the real qualities of the material thing. It is true indeed that when we speak of a thing's really having certain qualities we imply that it retains them even when, through the absence of the requisite causal conditions, it is not actually appearing to have them. But all that this involves is that the hypothetical propositions, which assert that the appear-

[1] Part IV.   [2] *Vide* Part V.

ances would be manifested if the conditions were fulfilled, remain true even when their protases happen not to be realized. It is true also, as Bradley says, that " if the qualities impart themselves never except under conditions ", we cannot say " what they are when unconditioned ". But the answer to this is that when we assert that a given quality really characterizes some material thing we are not asserting that it is unconditioned, in this sense. No doubt the argument would be valid if we conceived of material things as unobservable things-in-themselves. But we do not conceive of them in this way, and there is no good reason why we should.

In considering the use of the argument from illusion as a ground for distrusting the deliverances of sense-perception I may take as a text the famous passage in the *Meditations* of Descartes in which he explains how a wide experience by degrees sapped the faith which he had reposed in his senses. " For I frequently observed ", he says, " that towers which at a distance seemed round, appeared square when more closely viewed, and that colossal figures, raised on the summits of these towers, looked like small statues, when viewed from the bottom of them ; and in other instances without number, I also discovered errors in judgements founded on the external senses ; and not only in those founded on the external, but even in those that rested on the internal senses ; for is there aught more internal than pain ? And yet I have sometimes been informed by parties whose arm or leg had been amputated that they still occasionally seemed to feel pain in that part of the body which they had lost, a circumstance that led me to think that I could not be quite certain even that any one of my members was affected when I felt pain in it. And to these grounds of doubt I shortly afterwards added two others of very wide generality ; the first of them was that I believed I never perceived anything when awake which I could not occasionally think I also perceived when asleep, and as I do not believe that the ideas I seem to perceive in my sleep proceed from objects external to me, I did not any more observe any ground for believing this of such as I seem to perceive when awake ; the second was that since I was as yet ignorant of the author of my being, or at least supposed myself to be so, I saw nothing to prevent my having been so constituted by nature as that I should be deceived even in matters that appeared to me to possess the greatest truth. . . . And although the perceptions of the senses were not dependent on my will, I did not think that I ought on that ground to conclude that they proceeded from things different from myself, since perhaps there might be found in me some faculty, though hitherto unknown to me, which produced them." [1]

It is true that Descartes himself does not abide by these conclusions. But that is only because he thinks that he is able logically to demonstrate the existence of God, and that the assumption that the

[1] *Meditations on the First Philosophy*, Meditation VI, p. 131 of the Everyman edition.

teachings of the senses ought in general to be distrusted argues a deceitfulness in God which would be inconsistent with his goodness. And it is on this ground that he holds that " it is at least necessary to admit that all which I clearly and distinctly conceive as in [corporeal objects], that is, generally speaking, all that is comprehended in the object of speculative geometry, really exists external to me " ; [1] and also that " as I perceive different sorts of colours, sounds, odours, tastes, heat, hardness, etc., I safely conclude that there are in the bodies from which the diverse perceptions of the senses proceed certain varieties corresponding to them, although, perhaps, not in reality like them ".[2] His reasoning at this point is not, in my opinion, valid ; but we are not now concerned with the way in which he claimed to be able to overcome his distrust of his senses, but only with the question whether such a distrust is in any degree justified by the reasons that he gives.

The first thing to notice is that the errors of judgement to which Descartes refers are all of them errors of inference. The mere fact that a tower looks round from one standpoint and square from another need not be, and, in general, is not, a source of deception at all. If anyone is deceived by a fact of this kind, it is not merely because of the nature of his experiences, but because he bases an erroneous inference upon them. Let us take as an example the case of a man who, seeing the tower originally from a distance, assumed that he would always see

[1] *Op. cit.* p. 135.   [2] *Op. cit.* p. 126.

it as round. When he came close to it and found
that it then looked square, he would discover that
" his senses had deceived him ". But the reason
why he was deceived would be that he had assumed
that because an object presented a certain appearance
in one set of conditions, it would still present the
same appearance in another. In this particular
instance we should say that the man's assumption
was irrational as well as mistaken, inasmuch as it ran
counter to our experience of the way in which things
do alter their appearances. But even if the assumption had been rational, in this sense, it might still
have been false. And the same would apply to any
other judgement that involved an inference, whether
conscious or unconscious, from past to future experience. That is to say, the fallibility of the
senses is simply an instance of the fallibility of all
inductive reasoning. It consists in our being unable
formally to deduce the conclusion of an inductive
argument from its premises ; [1] and this is a necessary
fact, in the sense that the proposition which expresses
it is analytic. For an argument the premises [1] of
which did formally entail the conclusion would, by
definition, not be inductive. What is contingent is
the fact that some of the inductions that we make are

---

[1] In speaking of " the premises of an inductive argument " I
mean here to refer only to a set of singular propositions. I admit
that the particular conclusion of such an argument may follow
formally from its premises if these are taken to include some general
proposition. But the point is that this general proposition will not
itself be formally deducible from any set of singular propositions
that refer to the particular empirical facts in which alone the
evidence for it must ultimately consist.

actually unsuccessful ; but this does not affect the logical status of inductive reasoning. We may say indeed that the probability of the conclusions which we reach by inductive methods would, in general, be higher if these methods had never yet actually failed us. But the difference that this would make to the reliability of our judgements would be a difference of degree and not a difference of kind.

Exactly the same remarks apply to the errors in judgements " that rest on the internal senses ". The mistake that is made by the person who feels pain in an amputated limb is that of assuming that because such sensations of pain have previously been correlated with further tactual and visual experiences of a certain kind, the correlation must hold good in this case also. When he subsequently learns that these further experiences were not, in fact, obtainable, that in what would be described as normal conditions his leg would not have been visible or tangible at the time that he was feeling the pain, he realizes that his internal senses have deceived him. But here again his error is an error of inference, and one to which he would be theoretically subject even if he were never actually deceived. Perhaps it is the actual occurrence of such illusions that first calls our attention to the fallibility of perceptual judgements ; but it is not on this fact that their fallibility logically depends.

The case of dreams is not quite so simple. The argument here is that inasmuch as we often believe that we are having veridical perceptions when we are in fact dreaming, we can never be sure that we are not dreaming. To this many people will be content to reply, with Locke, that " if anyone will be so sceptical as to distrust his senses, and to affirm that all that we see and hear, feel and taste, think and do, during our whole being, is but the series and deluding appearance of a long dream whereof there is no reality ; and therefore will question the existence of all things or our knowledge of anything ; I must desire him to consider that if all be a dream, then he doth but dream that he makes the question ; and so it is not much matter that a waking man should answer him ".[1] But this rejoinder is more emotionally than intellectually convincing. It is true that if the man who says that all is a dream intends thereby to assert that all the propositions that anybody ever expresses are false, he cannot without contradiction include in this totality of false propositions the proposition which he is himself expressing. To suppose that he did so include it would be to extend to his case the familiar paradox of Epimenides the Cretan, who said that all Cretans were liars. It is, however, possible to deny any given proposition that is put forward without expressing one's denials in such a way that a proposition is ever used to negate itself. And in this fashion, assuming that the class of propositions denied is not itself inconsistent, a universal scepticism can be maintained without self-contradiction. Moreover, the view I am

---

[1] *An Essay concerning Human Understanding*, Book IV, ch. 2, section viii.

discussing is not that we are in fact living in a dream, but only that we cannot be sure that we are not; and to this Locke's objection does not apply. Nor is it satisfactory to say, as Locke also does, that " there is a very manifest difference between dreaming of being in the fire and being actually in it ". For it is not because they are intrinsically different from the sensations that we have when we are awake that we pronounce our dream sensations to be delusive, but rather because they do not fit into the general order of our experience. One remembers making certain perceptual judgements which were in accord with the experiences one was having at the time, but are not corroborated by one's present perceptions; and therefore one says that one must have been dreaming. But can I use a test of this kind to show that I am not still dreaming now? Does it prove anything more than that, if I am dreaming, the character of my dream is such that it is possible to discover among the experiences which constitute it a distinction analogous to that which is ordinarily drawn between veridical and delusive experiences? It does indeed sometimes happen that, in the course of a dream, one actually raises the question whether the perceptions one is having are veridical, and decides, reasonably but falsely, that they are. Can I then be sure that the experiences that I am now having are not part of a dream of this kind? And is there any reason why such a dream should not be indefinitely prolonged?

The answer is that if what is here meant by

" being sure " is " being able to give a conclusive
demonstration ", then it is true that I cannot at any
time be sure that I am not dreaming. I am able in
fact to convince myself that I am not, by putting my
perceptual judgements to the test of further experience and finding that they are substantiated. But
since there is no theoretical limit to this process of
testing, it is always logically possible that I am mistaken. However many favourable tests I may make,
the possibility still remains that my subsequent
experiences will consistently be such as to make me
conclude that the perceptions that I had to my own
satisfaction proved to be veridical were not so really,
and that I was dreaming after all. This question of
dreams is, indeed, only a special case of the general
problem that Descartes raises. Can we, in virtue of
our sense-experiences, ever be sure of the truth of
any proposition that implies the real existence of a
material thing ? Again the answer is that if what we
require to make us sure is a logical demonstration,
then we cannot ever be sure. Descartes himself con-
fuses the question by putting it in terms of a causal
theory of perception. He assumes that what we are
asserting when we assert a proposition implying the
existence of a material thing is that our perceptions
are produced by material things, which are themselves
not definable in phenomenal terms. But in fact, as I
shall argue later on, this is not what we ordinarily
mean by such propositions ; and, if it were, not only
should we not be able to demonstrate their truth ;
we should not even have any good inductive grounds

for believing them.[1] However, even if we correct this mistake of Descartes's and interpret propositions implying the existence of material things in a phenomenalistic fashion, the result, as regards the possibility of their demonstration, is the same. We do indeed verify many such propositions to an extent that makes it highly probable that they are true ; but since the series of relevant tests, being infinite, can never be exhausted, this probability can never amount to logical certainty. In this case also, the empirical fact that we sometimes have good reason to suppose that we actually are deceived is logically irrelevant to the argument. For even if all the propositions in question had hitherto been uniformly verified, this would not remove the possibility that future tests would give a consistently negative result. It would still further diminish the probability of this hypothesis, but with that I am not now concerned.

It must be admitted then that there is a sense in which it is true to say that we can never be sure, with regard to any proposition implying the existence of a material thing, that we are not somehow being deceived ; but at the same time one may object to this statement on the ground that it is misleading.[2] It is misleading because it suggests that the state of " being sure " is one the attainment of which is conceivable, but unfortunately not within our power. But, in fact, the conception of such a state is self-contradictory. For in order to be sure,

---

[1] Part IV.

[2] Cf. John Wisdom, " Philosophical Perplexity ", *Proceedings of the Aristotelian Society*, 1936–7.

in this sense, that we were not being deceived, we should have to have completed an infinite series of verifications ; and it is an analytic proposition that one cannot run through all the members of an infinite series. Nor would the situation be different if our beliefs concerning material things were founded, not upon sense-perception, but rather, as Descartes suggested, upon some " intuition of the mind ". For we could not conceivably have the means of demonstrating that any such intuition was infallible. Accordingly, what we should say, if we wish to avoid misunderstanding, is not that we can never be certain that any of the propositions in which we express our perceptual judgements are true, but rather that the notion of certainty does not apply to propositions of this kind. It applies to the *a priori* propositions of logic and mathematics, and the fact that it does apply to them is an essential mark of distinction between them and empirical propositions. But once this is recognized, the motive for scepticism has gone. The mistake of the sceptic is not that he maintains any falsehood, or doubts some self-evident truth, but that he insists on applying to one class of propositions a criterion that is appropriate only to another. The positive result of his argument is to call our attention to the fact that the relationship of propositions describing the contents of our sense-experiences to propositions implying the existence of material things is not that of premises to conclusion in a deductive argument. Our procedure in such cases is always inductive, and it remains inductive however much sensible evidence we may accumulate. This may indeed be regarded as a truism ; but it is all that the argument I have been examining shows.

5. Theories of Perception as Alternative Languages

The final use of the argument from illusion which I have to consider is that which is supposed to refute the perceptual theory of Naïve Realism. And for this I cannot do better than refer to Professor Price's book on *Perception*.[1] According to him, what is to be understood by Naïve Realism is the thesis that visual and tactual sense-data are parts of the surfaces of material things ; which, since he defines a sense-datum as that which is immediately given in perception, is equivalent to the thesis that it is always a material thing that we see or touch. And he maintains that if the argument from illusion proves nothing else, it does at least refute this thesis. But this is a question with which I have already dealt ; and I have shown that the answer depends upon the way in which the thesis is interpreted. If one assumes that the naïve realist is using the words " see " and " touch " in such a way that to say of an object that it is seen or touched does not entail saying that it exists or that it really has the properties that it appears to have, then it is clear that the argument from illusion cannot be used to refute him. If, on the other hand, he is using these words in a way that does carry these

[1] Ch. ii.

implications, then the argument does refute him, so
long as he adheres in other respects to our ordinary
usage of words. But if he is prepared to modify
this usage and introduce suitable conventions with
regard to the variability of material things, then, as
we have seen, it is possible for him consistently to
maintain his position without running counter to the
empirical facts.

A third possibility, which is suggested by Price's
formulation of the thesis, is that it should be interpreted as a theory about the analysis of material
things in terms of sense-data. According to this
interpretation, what the naïve realist is asserting is
that " A is perceiving x ", where x stands for a
material thing, can be analysed into " A is sensing a
sense-datum and knowing it to be part of the surface
of x ". And this can indeed be refuted by means of
the argument from illusion. For we can say to the
naïve realist : " You say that perceiving a material
thing can be analysed into sensing a sense-datum and
knowing that it is part of the surface of a material
thing. But is it not significant to say that the sense-
datum by means of which A is perceiving a coin is
round, and that the sense-datum by means of which
B is perceiving the same coin is elliptical ? And
would it not be self-contradictory to say that a part
of the surface of a coin was both elliptical and
round ? "

As an argument *ad hominem* this may be decisive.
But all that it proves is that the naïve realist's thesis
is inconsistent with the conventions of the sense-

datum language ; so that if we refute him by interpreting his thesis in terms of sense-data we are begging the question against him. It is indeed misleading to speak of refutation at all in this context, unless we assume that the naïve realist is merely denying that there are illusions ; and I do not think that any philosopher has really intended to deny this empirical fact. For my argument has shown that if we do not make this unwarranted assumption we have to regard the thesis of naïve realism, not as an assertion of fact, but as a proposal to use words in a certain fashion ; and the same is true, as we have seen, of the thesis that we experience sense-data. If we accept the sense-datum terminology, then we must reject the terminology of naïve realism ; for the two are mutually incompatible. But this is not to say that we regard the theory of sense-data as true and the theory of naïve realism as false. For I have shown that these so-called theories of perception are not theories at all in the ordinary sense, and therefore that the notions of truth and falsehood, which we apply to scientific theories, are not applicable to them.

To illustrate further this important point that what philosophers call theories of perception are not theories at all, in the scientific sense, I may refer once again to Price's book. In a chapter which he entitles " Some Modifications of Naïve Realism ", he examines " three ways in which philosophers have attempted to modify the Naïve Realist thesis, so as to make it defensible ". These he calls " The

Theory of Multiple Location ", which he attributes
to Professor Whitehead, " The Theory of Compound
Things ", which he attributes to Professor Alex-
ander, and " The Theory of Appearing ", which he
attributes to Professor Prichard and Professor G. E.
Moore. The hypothesis which is said to be contained
in the Theory of Multiple Location is that, besides
the properties " which characterize it *simpliciter* ",
a material thing also has properties " which characterize it only from a place " ; and these properties
belong to it just as truly and objectively as the others.
" The penny just *is* elliptical from this and that place
and kinked from such and such others ; exactly as
in itself (and from certain specially favoured places)
it is circular and smooth in outline." [1] To this
Price raises the objection that the theory does not
meet the cases of double vision and complete hallucination. He maintains that it will not do to say
that a thing is doubled from a certain place, " for
' doubleness ' is not a quality at all ".[2] Nor is
" hallucinatoriness " a quality. When we say that
a perception of a material thing is hallucinatory, we
are not saying that the thing either has or appears to
have a peculiar property ; what we are saying is that
there really is no such thing. The same objections
are held to apply to the Theory of Compound
Things, according to which " illusory visual and
tactual sense-data do really form parts of the surface
of an object, but of a compound object. The stick is
not bent, but the compound stick-plus-water really is

[1] *Perception*, pp. 55-6.   [2] P. 57.

bent, and the crooked sense-datum is part of its surface. These compound objects really do exist in external Nature and do have their qualities just as ' simple ' objects like sticks have theirs." [1] Professor Price remarks that, to be consistent, the exponents of this theory ought to include among the constituents of their compound objects " the sense-organs and brain of the observer " ; [2] for they also affect the nature of what is experienced ; and in that case every object that we see or touch will be compound, in the sense in which this word is here being used. But is this a proper sense ? asks Professor Price. Surely all that there really is, is a group of causally related objects. If they formed a compound " it ought to be possible to point to at least one attribute possessed by all of them in common and not by any of them in isolation — for instance, a characteristic shape or mass or inertia, or some such causal property as serves to distinguish a chemical compound from other compounds and from its own constituents. But no such attribute can be found." [3] And finally, he objects that even if there were such compound objects, the theory would not save Naïve Realism ; for they would be very different from the material things that we ordinarily suppose that we observe.

With regard to the Theory of Appearing, we are told that it consists in taking what we see or touch to be always " a part of an object's surface appearing to someone to have certain characteristics. On one

[1] *Ibid.* 58-9.   [2] P. 59.   [3] P. 61.

form of the theory ' appearing ' is the name of a
unique and unanalysable three-term relation between
a part of an object's surface, a characteristic or set of
characteristics, and a certain mind. On another
form of it, ' *A* appears *b* to *S* ' stands for a unique
and unanalysable kind of fact about *A-b*-ness and
S's mind ".[1] Professor Price allows that this theory
can deal with such straightforward phenomena as
distortions of perspective and colour ; but he maintains that it cannot account for the cases, such as
those of double vision and complete hallucination,
where there is a transition " from qualitative appearing to existential appearing ". For in these cases
there exists no material thing to be a term of the
unanalysable relation, or an ingredient in the unanalysable fact.

Now the point which here again seems to have
escaped both the exponents of these " theories " and
their critic is that, as the word is ordinarily understood, they are not alternative theories at all. This
may become clear if I employ the method of comparison. Suppose, for example, that we are looking
for a theory to account for the nature of our dreams.
Then one hypothesis which we may consider is that
they correspond to physical stimuli ; another is that
they are prognostications of future waking experiences ; another, that they are the expressions of
unconscious wishes and fears. To decide which is
the most probable we apply them to the empirical
facts. We then find that although there are

[1] P. 62.

experiences that favour the first of these theories, as when one dreams of being naked and wakes to find that the blankets have slipped, or when a dream experience of the sound of church bells merges into a waking experience of the ringing of an alarm-clock, yet even in these exceptional cases the theory does not cover the details of our dreams ; and in general it provides no explanation for the variety and diversity of their contents. Similarly, we find that the correspondences that have so far been discovered between people's dreams and their subsequent waking experiences are too few and uncertain to provide a basis for any generalization on which we can rely. On the other hand, the empirical evidence that psycho-analysts have collected in favour of the third theory is comparatively strong ; and it has been confirmed by the success with which, on being applied to the treatment of nervous disorders, it leads to the detection of " unconscious experiences ". If, therefore, we decide that the theory that our dreams are the expressions of unconscious wishes and fears is the most probable of the three, it is because we find that we are able to deduce from it a greater proportion of the known empirical facts, and because by its means we are able to make more reliable inferences from the known to the unknown.

Pursuing this comparison, let us accordingly attempt to apply those three so-called theories of perception, " the theory of multiple location ", " the theory of compound things ", and " the theory of

appearing ", to the empirical facts. Can we discover
any empirical evidence that favours any one of these
theories rather than another, in the sense in which
the evidence put forward by the psycho-analysts
favours their theory of dreams ? The answer is that
the comparison at once breaks down. For we find
that every conceivable experience, in the field to
which these theories refer, can equally well be sub-
sumed under any of them. Each of them will cover
any known fact ; but none of them, on the other
hand, enables us to make any inference at all from
the known to the unknown. No matter which of
them we adopted, we should be able to describe our
perceptions, whatever their nature ; what we should
not be able to do would be to make any predictions.
But if the relation of these three theories to the
relevant phenomena is precisely the same, then, as
theories, they are not distinguishable from one
another. And if they allow no possibility of extra-
polation, if the actual course of our experience can
have no bearing upon their truth or falsehood, it is
misleading to call them theories at all.

At this point it may be objected that our experience may very well be relevant to the validity of
these theories. For have we not seen that the ground
upon which Professor Price rejects them is that they
fail to account for such phenomena as those of double
vision and complete hallucination ? And does not
this show that they are capable of being empirically
tested, and that they do not all describe all the known
facts, but are incompatible with some of them? This

indeed is the opinion one would derive from a casual reading of Price's arguments. But when one comes to examine them more closely, one finds that his objections are purely linguistic. We have seen, for example, that he rejects the " theory of multiple location " on the ground that one cannot say that a material thing has the quality of being double or being hallucinatory from a certain place, since being double and being hallucinatory are not qualities. But this is an objection only to the form of certain sentences and not to their content. A slight emenda-.tion is all that is necessary to meet it. Instead of saying that a material thing M really is double or hallucinatory from a place P, the exponents of the theory will have to say that there are two M's from P, or in the case of an hallucination, that there is an M from P but not from other places. Similarly, the exponents of the " theory of appearing ", instead of saying that a thing appears double to a given observer, will have to say that there appear to him to be two things ; nor need they be disturbed by the objection that in the case of a complete hallucination there really is no material thing to be a term for the relation of appearing ; for they can answer that their use of the word " appear " is such that in saying that a material thing appears to someone they do not imply that it exists ; and indeed this is not an abnormal usage of the word. In the case of the " theory of compound things " the linguistic char-acter of Price's objection is still more obvious; for what his arguments amount to is merely that the

word " compound " is being used in an unfamiliar
sense. But to refute a theory something more is
required than criticisms of the manner in which it is
formulated. The essential question is not whether
the theory is expressed in a way that conforms to
our ordinary verbal conventions, but whether it fits
the empirical facts.

It must be said then that if the " theories "
against which they are directed really were theories,
in the sense in which this word is commonly understood, Professor Price's objections would be without
force. But the truth is not that his objections are
without force, but that he has mistaken the character
of that which he is attempting to refute. For what
he regards as alternative theories are, in fact, what I
should call alternative languages. As languages, they
afford us the means of describing what we already
know, but it is not to be expected that we should be
able to deduce anything from them concerning the
nature of our future experience ; for if that were
possible they would not be languages, but theories
in the ordinary sense. Nor is it to be expected that
we should be able to discover any factual objections
to them. For what we here have to consider is not
a number of alternative hypotheses concerning the
nature of the empirical facts, but a number of
alternative recommendations concerning the way in
which we are to describe them. And whether or not
we are to accept any of these recommendations is a
question that we have to decide on linguistic grounds.

A feature which the " theories " of multiple

location and compound things have in common with the " theory " of sense-data, which has been adopted in one form or another by most modern philosophers, is that they all recommend that we should make some departure from our ordinary mode of speech. In this they differ from the " theory of appearing ", which may indeed be interpreted as being simply the proposal that we should continue to describe perceptual situations in the way that we ordinarily do. Now I have shown that there is no ground for supposing that acceptance of this proposal would make it impossible to give a truthful description of any empirical matter of fact ; so that if I reject it, in philosophizing about perception, it is not because the " theory of appearing " is false, but because I regard the alternative language of sense-data as being more suitable for my purpose. And this applies also to my rejection of the "theories" of compound things and multiple location. The forms of expression which are advocated in these theories are intended, like that of the sense-datum theory, to eliminate the problems which arise out of the ambiguous use of words like " touch " and " see " in ordinary speech ; but they do not achieve this in a satisfactory way. What makes the " theory of multiple location " inadequate in this respect is chiefly the fact that variations in the appearances of material things do not depend merely on the position of the observer, but also on many other factors which the theory does not specify. They are indeed specified in the " theory of compound things " : but this very virtue makes its terminology too cumbersome to be convenient. There is, moreover, a further objection to both these alternatives to the sense-datum terminology, in that they lack the advantage, which the other affords, of enabling us to refer to the contents of our sense-experiences, without referring to material things.

Accordingly, I may sum up my long discussion of the argument from illusion by saying that it makes it seem desirable to use a technical terminology of some kind in philosophizing about perception ; and that of those that are available the terminology of the " sense-datum theory " appears to be the best. But it must be understood clearly that the acceptance of this theory involves nothing more than a decision to use a technical language ; and I shall attempt to specify the conventions of this language more precisely than has been the custom of those who have used it hitherto. For otherwise it will be found to defeat its own object by giving rise to a number of fictitious problems, which are no less troublesome than those that it enables us to escape.

II

THE CHARACTERIZATION OF SENSE-DATA

6. ACTS AND OBJECTS IN SENSATION

I HAVE not so far attempted to give any explicit definition of the word " sense-datum ". I have chosen rather to indicate its usage by giving examples in which sentences referring to sense-data are introduced as translations of sentences the meaning of which is already known. The general rule which one may derive from these examples is that the propositions we ordinarily express by saying that a person A is perceiving a material thing M, which appears to him to have the quality x, may be expressed in the sense-datum terminology by saying that A is sensing a sense-datum s, which really has the quality x, and which belongs to M. In this case it is assumed that the word " perceive ", or whatever word may be employed to designate the kind of perceiving that is in question, is being used in such a way that to say that a material thing M is perceived entails saying that it exists. If we do not make this assumption, then we must say not that s belongs to M but only that A takes it to belong to M, and so allow for the possibility that M does not exist ; but in other respects the translation is the same. And from this it follows that to assert that people actually do experience sense-data need be to assert no more than that such propositions as that I am now perceiving a clock or a pen or a table, in a sense of " perceiving " that does not necessarily entail that these objects exist, are sometimes true. And I do not see how it can be denied, not merely that many propositions of this kind are in fact true, but also that we often have good reason to suppose that they are. I can therefore claim to be using the word " sense-datum " in such a way that there can be no serious doubt that sense-data actually are experienced.

In following this procedure, I shall, I think, be giving to the word " sense-datum " the meaning that the philosophers who have adopted the " theory of sense-data " have, in general, intended it to have, though I shall show that some of them have also been inclined to make statements about sense-data that are inconsistent with this usage. And the definition of sense-data that these philosophers commonly give is that they are the objects of which, in sense-perception, one is directly aware. By this they must be understood to mean, not that only those objects of which someone is in fact directly aware are to be called sense-data, but rather that the word " sense-datum " is to stand for any object of which it is conceivable that someone should be directly aware. They do not always say this ; but inasmuch as they consider themselves entitled to refer to possible as well as to actual sense-data, it may fairly be assumed that this is what they mean.

The first criticism that I have to make of this definition is that it is not illuminating. For there is no accepted meaning of the expression " direct awareness " by reference to which it can be made clear without further explanation what is to be meant by the word " sense-datum ". I think that we should ordinarily say that we were directly aware of any object, our belief in the existence of which was based upon sense-experience and did not involve any conscious process of inference. But if the expression " direct awareness " is used in this sense, then it will be true to say that we are directly aware of material things, such as chairs and tables and pens. For although our beliefs in the existence of such things are inductive, in the sense that they imply more than would be implied by a mere description of the experiences on which they are based, they often do not involve any conscious process of inference. The proposition that I am holding a pen in my hand is not equivalent to any proposition or set of pro-positions that describe my present sense-experiences, though they provide me with the only grounds I have for asserting it. But this does not mean that I have consciously gone through any process of inferring it from them. In virtue of my sense-experiences I simply take it for granted that this is a pen. And this is the way in which we actually arrive at a great many of our beliefs in the existence of material things. But, as a rule, those who define sense-data as the objects of which one can be directly aware maintain that one cannot be directly aware of such objects as tables or pens. And the reason why they maintain this is that our perception of such things may always be delusive. In other words, they define " direct awareness " in such a way that if someone is directly aware of an object x, it follows that x exists and that it really has whatever properties it is appearing to have. But having given this meaning to the propositional function " A is directly aware of x ", where, it may be asked, are they to find values that will satisfy it ? The answer is that they provide these values by introducing the word " sense-datum ", or some synonymous term, and using it in the way that I have indicated. That is to say, the expressions " direct awareness " and " sense-datum " are to be regarded as correlative ; and since each of them is being used in a special, technical sense, it is not satisfactory merely to define one in terms of the other. It is necessary first to employ some other method, such as the method of giving examples, in order to show how one or other of them is to be understood.

This definition of sense-data as the objects of direct awareness is often associated with a particular view about the analysis of sensations which it does not logically entail. This view is that it is possible to discriminate in any sensation at least two distinct factors, one of them being the act of sensing and the other the object sensed. I say that the acceptance of the definition does not entail the acceptance of this analysis of sensation, because it is clearly possible to assert that we are directly aware of sense-data without implying that the expression " direct awareness " is a name for any sort of introspectible act. And indeed it seems to me very doubtful whether there are such acts. It is true, as Professor G. E. Moore points out in his " Refutation of Idealism ",[1] that the expressions " blue " and " consciousness of blue " are not synonymous, and that my consciousness of blue and my consciousness of green have something more in common than what is common to blue and green. But it does not follow that this common element of consciousness is a distinct, individual factor in any sensation. It may well be that the characteristic in virtue of which it may be said that the blue and green sense-data are both experienced by me is a relational characteristic, which does not involve either myself, conceived as a substance, or any such thing as that for which the expression " act of sensing " is supposed to be a name, but only certain other sensible, or introspectible, objects. And whether such an analysis is correct or not, there is nothing in Moore's argument to refute it.

There are, however, some philosophers who base their belief in the existence of these acts of sensing, not on any *a priori* argument, but on the evidence of their own introspection ; and I do not wish to assert dogmatically that they are wrong. I cannot myself discover these acts by introspection ; but this does not prove that no one else can. At the same time, I

---

[1] *Philosophical Studies*, pp. 7-30.

think that those who do claim to be able to discover them in this way may, perhaps, be making an unwarranted inference from a different empirical fact. It is characteristic of some sense-data that they appear to be sensibly outside ourselves ; by which I mean only that they occur in sense-fields that have the property of sensible depth. This is true of visual and tactual data, and also of auditory and olfactory data when they are ascribed to an objective source. Now, because of our knowledge of their immediate causal conditions, we tend to think of our sensations as occurring somehow inside ourselves ; and therefore it is assumed that sense-data that are at a distance from the somatic centres of their sense-fields, and thus may be said to be sensibly outside ourselves, cannot make up the whole content of the corresponding sensations ; and so acts of sensing are brought in to fill the gap. If this explanation were correct, we should expect to find that those who made this distinction between act and object in their analysis of sensation were more confident of its validity in respect of sight and touch than in respect of organic and kinæsthetic sensations ; and this is, in fact, the case.[1] But it is clear that if those who believe in the existence of acts of sensing are tacitly relying on this argument, their conclusion is not established. The most that they can prove is that some sensations are not identical with the relevant sense-data, or in other words that the expression " sensation of x " is not synonymous with " x ".

---

[1] Cf. C. D. Broad, *Scientific Thought*, pp. 254-7.

But while we might conclude from this that in asserting that a sense-datum was experienced, we were asserting that it was related to something other than itself, it would not follow that this other term was an act of sensing. For, as I have already remarked, there is no logical inconsistency in holding both that " the sensation of x " is not synonymous with " x ", and also that the proposition that the act of sensing is a distinct, individual factor in any sensation is empirically false.

However, the philosophers who maintain this distinction between act and object in their analysis of sensation do not, for the most part, desire merely to call attention to an empirical matter of fact. They consider the distinction to be philosophically important because they think that they can use it to refute Berkeleyan idealism. For, according to Berkeley, colours and shapes and sounds and all other " sensible qualities " are mind-dependent, inasmuch as their existence consists in their being perceived ; and since material things are, in his view, nothing but collections of sensible qualities, he concludes that they too cannot exist apart from a perceiving mind.[1] But here, it is argued, he falls into error through failing to distinguish between the object of a sensation and the act. Acts of sensation, it is said, are indeed mind-dependent; but it does not follow that their objects are ; for there is no good ground for supposing that the object of a

---

[1] Vide *A Treatise concerning the Principles of Human Knowledge* and *Three Dialogues between Hylas and Philonous, passim.*

sensation cannot exist apart from the act. And if we assume, as some philosophers do, that these acts of sensation are acts of knowing, then it is held that we can go so far as to maintain that the objects of our sensations *must* exist independently of the acts ; for it is supposed to be an essential characteristic of knowledge that what is known exists independently of the knowing of it. But this argument is two-edged, as Professor Prichard has recently shown.[1] For he maintains that it is self-evident that the existence of what he calls secondary qualities and I should call sense-data, does depend upon their being perceived, in Berkeley's sense of the word ; and therefore that the proper conclusion of the foregoing argument is not that the objects of our sensations exist independently of the acts, but that acts of sensation are not acts of knowing. And since he supposes, with some historical justification, that sense-data are defined as the objects of perceptual acts which are taken to be acts of knowing, he concludes that there are no such things as sense-data. For he argues that to say that there are sense-data is simply a misleading way of saying that " perceiving is a kind of knowing ", and that this proposition is false.

7. " Esse est Percipi "

But, setting aside for the moment the question whether perceiving, in the sense here in point, is or

[1] In a paper called " The Sense-datum Fallacy ", *Aristotelian Society Supplementary Proceedings*, 1938.

is not a kind of knowing, I wish first of all to examine the Berkeleyan principle that to exist is to be perceived. I shall consider it first in relation to material things, and then in relation to sense-data. And here it must be understood that in using the term " sense-datum " I am not presupposing that " sensible qualities " are objects of knowledge, in Prichard's sense ; nor am I making any other covert assumption. My use of the term is so far to be understood only by reference to the examples that I have given ; and whatever further implications I intend it to carry, I shall explicitly introduce.

If the principle that *esse est percipi*, as applied to material things, is to be interpreted to mean that a logical contradiction is involved in asserting the existence of any material thing that is not actually being perceived, then it is plainly false. For even if it is the case that no propositions asserting the existence of unperceived material things are, in fact, ever true, they are still not self-contradictory. But is it the case that no such propositions are true ? It has indeed been argued that we can never have any reason to believe in their truth, on the ground that the only evidence we can have for the existence of a material thing is that we actually perceive it, and that it is impossible to perceive something existing unperceived.[1] But this argument is invalid. It is true that if we were to regard the existence of material things as being logically independent, not merely of actual perceptions, but also of all possible

[1] Cf. W. T. Stace, " The Refutation of Realism ", *Mind*, 1934.

perceptions, then we should have no good reason to believe that they ever existed unperceived. But this is not an acceptable analysis. The criterion by which we determine that a material thing exists is the truth of various hypothetical propositions asserting that if certain conditions were fulfilled we should perceive it.[1] These propositions cannot indeed be formally deduced from the propositions which describe the contents of our actual perceptions. But they can be derived from them by an ordinary inductive argument. We may say, therefore, that we are justified in believing that material things exist when no one is actually perceiving them, because the fact that we do constantly perceive them in certain conditions gives us a good inductive ground for believing, at times when we are not perceiving them, that we should be perceiving them if these conditions were fulfilled. If the conditions are not, in fact, fulfilled, then we cannot put our belief to a direct empirical test. But this does not mean that it is baseless. For, as I have already remarked, it is not required for the validity of the hypothetical propositions about sense-data, in terms of which one can analyse propositions about material things,[2] that their protases should be empirically realized. And it is this that constitutes the independence of material things. Accordingly, I conclude that it is not a necessary condition of the existence of a material thing, or for our belief in its existence to be justifiable, that it should actually be

---

[1] For an explanation of this see Part V of this book.
[2] Cf. Part V.

perceived. Nor is it an altogether sufficient condition. For I am using the word " perception " in such a way that it is possible for a perception to be delusive.

In reaching this conclusion that the existence of material things is to be determined with reference to possible rather than actual perceptions, I have been guided by the way in which the relevant words are currently used. But this is not a method that one can extend to the case of sense-data. For here the problem is not to elucidate the conventions that govern the use of an existing language, but to formulate conventions for an artificial language. In the case of material things, one is able to make use of a previous understanding of the meaning of existential propositions in order to criticize the principle that to exist is to be perceived. But in the case of sense-data one has no such previous understanding. The position in this case is that one must decide whether to accept or reject this principle in order to determine what one is going to mean by saying that a sense-datum exists.

Now one of the purposes which the introduction of the sense-datum terminology is intended to serve is that it should enable us to deal with the problems which arise from the fact that material things can appear to have qualities that they do not really have, and can appear to exist when they do not. It is this that is effected by the translation of such sentences as " I am perceiving a brown carpet, which looks yellow to me " or " The drunkard sees

animals which are not really there " into " I am
sensing a yellow sense-datum which belongs to a
brown carpet " or " The drunkard sees sense-data
which he takes to belong to animals, but which do
not really belong to anything ". The advantage of
this procedure is that it makes it possible for us to say
that something real is being experienced even in cases
where our perceptions are delusive. But this advantage is sacrificed if we extend the distinction
between appearance and reality to sense-data themselves. And for this reason we should not allow any
meaning to such sentences as " I am sensing a yellow
sense-datum, but it is really brown " or " Perhaps
the sense-data that I am now sensing do not really
exist ". It is true that some philosophers have been
inclined to attach meaning to sentences of this kind.
They have seriously considered the possibility that
sense-data as well as material things might appear to
have properties they did not really have. And it
may be argued that this is simply a question of an
alternative specification of the rules of the sense-
datum language, and that they are free to adopt such
a convention if they wish. But the answer is that by
adopting this convention they come to treat sense-
data as if they were themselves material things or
characteristics of material things ; and in that case
the terminology of sense-data becomes superfluous.
The point of introducing it was to clarify the meaning
of the sentences in which we ordinarily refer to
material things by using a language of a different
structure from that of our ordinary language. But

if the reference to sense-data is to serve this purpose, it is necessary that the criteria that determine the proper use of such sentences as " this sense-datum is brown " should be different from those that determine the proper use of such sentences as " this carpet is brown ". If we make them the same, our new terminology becomes a mere reproduction of the old. It eliminates none of the familiar problems, and so far from being a source of clarification, it creates additional confusion by suggesting that the introduction of sense-data is not just a linguistic expedient, but marks the discovery of a new kind of material thing.

We must decide therefore not to admit the distinction between veridical and delusive perception with regard to sense-data. And this means that we must make it a sufficient condition of the existence of a sense-datum that it should actually be sensed. But are we also to make it a necessary condition ? A conceivable objection to this is that we wish to speak not merely of actual but also of possible sense-data ; for in analysing propositions about material things we have to refer, not so much to the sense-experiences we are actually having, as to those that we should be having if certain hypothetical conditions were fulfilled. And it may be argued that, in so far as these hypothetical propositions are true, we must allow that possible sense-data, or sensibilia, as Bertrand Russell called them,[1] also exist without necessarily being experienced. But there is really no reason why we should draw this conclusion. We do

[1] Vide *Mysticism and Logic*, pp. 148 ff.

indeed make the truth of these hypothetical propositions a criterion for the existence of material things,
but it is not necessary that we should extend this
procedure to the case of sense-data. The convenience
of our use of the word " existence " as applied to
material things consists in the indefiniteness and the
generality of its reference. It enables us to assert a
number of hypothetical propositions about the contents of our sense-experiences without having to
specify them individually. But no such advantage
is to be obtained from the proposed usage of
" existence " in connexion with possible sense-data.
For if we are to avoid identifying these sensibilia with
material things we shall have to take as a criterion for
the existence of a sensibile the truth of a single
hypothetical proposition ; and in that case we shall
be able to express no more by asserting that the
sensibile exists than we are already able to express
by asserting the hypothetical proposition in question.
And not only is there no positive advantage in
extending the use of the word " existence " in this
way to possible sense-data ; there is also the dis-
advantage that the proposed usage, though not indeed
identical with that which is adopted in connexion
with material things, is sufficiently like it to be a ready
source of confusion. Accordingly, I find it advisable
to make it a necessary as well as a sufficient condition
of the existence of sense-data that they should in
fact be sensed. I shall continue to speak of possible sense-data as an alternative way of asserting
the relevant hypothetical propositions. But only

sense-data that are actually experienced will be said to exist.

It may be noted that this decision to accept the principle that the existence of sense-data consists in their being experienced involves neither an admission nor a denial of the distinction between acts of sensation and their objects ; and so a refutation of the principle that consists merely in an attempt to establish this distinction cannot have any validity for us. Moreover, it seems that those who seek to " refute idealism " in this way are making the mistake of treating the question whether the existence of sense-data consists in their being experienced, not as a question concerning the rules of the sense-datum language, but as a question of fact. Professor G. E. Moore, for example, in his " Refutation of Idealism ",[1] expressly asserts that he regards *esse est percipi* as a synthetic proposition. From this it may be inferred that he is using the word " existence " in a different sense from that in which I have decided to use it in connexion with sense-data, but he does not tell us what this sense is. He asserts dogmatically that the sentences " blue exists " and " the consciousness of blue exists " do not express equivalent propositions, and suggests that the failure to see this is mainly responsible for the groundless belief that *esse est percipi*. But while it is fairly clear from the context that he is using the word " blue " to mean what I should call a blue sense-datum, it is not at all clear how he is using the word " exists ".

[1] *Philosophical Studies*, pp. 1-30.

If the sense intended is that in which the word is applied to material things, then, as I have shown, he is right in maintaining that not everything that exists must also be in fact perceived. But I have shown also that the effect of extending this usage of " existence " to sense-data is to make the sense-datum terminology superfluous. There is no point in talking about sense-data at all unless we adopt rules for the use of this technical term that are different from the rules we already follow in speaking about material things. And for this reason it is not legitimate to assume, as Moore apparently does, that a question which has a factual meaning with reference to material things must also have a factual meaning when it is made to refer to sense-data. This is not, of course, to say that no true factual statements can be made about sense-data, but only that it is advisable, if one is going to express empirical propositions with the help of this technical term, to begin by having a clear understanding of what is involved in its use.

To show how the neglect of this point can lead to confusion, I may refer to another article by Moore which he entitles " Some Judgements of Perception ".[1] In this he maintains that it is quite certain that when one makes such a judgement as that " this is an inkstand ", there is one and only one object about which one is making this judgement, though the judgement one is making about it is certainly not that it is itself a whole inkstand, and that this object

---

[1] *Ibid.* pp. 220-52.

is a sense-datum. He then raises the question how this sense-datum is related to the inkstand, and says that he is inclined to adopt the view that it is literally part of it. He admits that in order to maintain this he must also hold that sense-data can sometimes appear to have qualities that they do not really have, and that this supposition is one that is often thought to be nonsensical. He says, however, that he is not himself convinced that it is nonsensical. But now we must ask why it should be thought to be certain that a judgement such as " this is an inkstand " is really about a sense-datum. Why should it not be about an inkstand ? The answer is that the judgement is held not to be about the inkstand because it is assumed that the inkstand itself is not sensibly " given ". There is indeed a familiar use of the word " about " according to which it would be proper to say that the judgement " this is an inkstand " really was about an inkstand. But this is not the way in which Moore is using the word. He is using it in such a way that to say that a judgement is about an object x entails that x is given, in a sense in which sense-data can be said to be given but inkstands cannot. But what exactly is this sense ? Why may we not say that inkstands are given, rather than sense-data ? It is because the perception which gives rise to our judgement that " this is an inkstand " may always be qualitatively or existentially delusive. There may not really be an inkstand there, or it may not really have the qualities that it appears to have on this occasion. But if this is the reason why Moore holds that the inkstand is not sensibly given, then it is clear that he cannot consistently allow that the sense-datum, which is supposed by him to be that which the judgement is really about, may itself appear to have qualities that it does not really have. For in saying that the judgement that " this is an inkstand " is really not about an inkstand but about a sense-datum, which is a way of saying that it is not the inkstand but only a sense-datum that is sensibly given, he is implying that the perception of sense-data cannot be delusive in the sense in which the perception of an inkstand can. If, therefore, he maintains that the sense-datum as well as the ink-stand can appear to have qualities that it does not really have, he falls into self-contradiction. He is not entitled to assume that because the distinction between veridical and delusive perception applies to material things, it applies also to sense-data. For this assumption is inconsistent with the way in which he intends that the word " sense-datum " should be used.

We have seen that the reason why some philos-ophers have been anxious to deny that the existence even of sense-data consists in their being perceived, is that the acceptance of this principle is thought to lead to idealism. It is believed that if we admit that the objects of which we are directly aware can exist only when we are experiencing them, we shall be committed to the view that everything that we experience " exists only in the mind ", and that this is to put in question the reality of the external world.

But what is meant here by saying that an object exists in the mind ? Presumably that it is what we should ordinarily call a state of mind. But in that case the proposition that sense-data exist only in the mind does not follow from the proposition that they cannot exist unsensed. To say that a colour or a sound or any other sense-datum exists only when it is experienced does not by any means entail saying that it is a state of mind, in the ordinary sense in which a feeling or an emotion is held to be a state of mind. And indeed there appears to be no good reason for holding that any such sense-data are states of mind, in this sense.

But if the assertion that sense-data exist only in the mind is not to be understood in this way, how are we to interpret it ? I do not think that it is possible to find any satisfactory meaning for it, unless we assume that it is merely a misleading way of re-stating the convention that the existence of sense-data is to consist in their being experienced ; but at the same time we can, I think, account for its being made. For what we have here is yet another instance of the misuse of the argument from illusion. In this case the argument is taken to prove that the objects of which we are sensibly aware do not form part of an external, material world. Nevertheless it is assumed that since these objects are undeniably experienced they must in some sense be real ; and as they have been extruded from the material world, it is thought that another receptacle must be found for them ; and the only one that appears to be available is the mind. How indeed the mind is supposed to contain them, it is not easy to understand. I do not think that even Berkeley can really have wished to maintain that " sensible qualities " were literally inherent in the mind as in a region of space. Nevertheless he was sufficiently misled by the spatial metaphor to be capable of arguing, in support of his view that we have no direct visual perception of distance, that the extension and figure of an object seem to be in the same place as its colour, and that the colours that we see cannot be at a distance from us because it is " agreed on all hands, by those who have any thoughts of that matter, that colours, which are the proper and immediate object of sight, are not without the mind ".[1] But, apart from such absurdities as this, the whole process of reasoning that leads to the attempt to house sense-data in the mind is thoroughly confused. For, in the first place, I have shown that the argument from illusion does not prove that the objects of which we are sensibly aware are not constituents of the material world, if this is regarded as a question of fact. It does indeed provide us with a motive for altering our terminology in a way that results in our saying that we are directly aware, not of material things, but only of sense-data. But this means that we are adopting a new method of describing our perceptual experience, which is a substitute for our ordinary method of description and cannot simply be grafted upon it. To ask

[1] *A New Theory of Vision*, section xliii.

whether sense-data inhere in the material world or in the mind is thus entirely to misconceive their character. If we agree to say that the objects of which we are directly aware are always sense-data, then we are deciding to treat them and not minds or material things as the units in terms of which we are to describe our perceptual experience. The question, therefore, that we must ask is not how sense-data are to be incorporated in the categories of mind or matter, or whereabouts they are to be located in physical space, but rather how our conceptions of " mind " and " material things " and " physical space " are to be analysed in terms of them. Accordingly, if we conclude that sense-data are not states of mind, we must not then look round for some other container for them, such as the brain or " the psycho-cerebral compound ". For it is already a mistake to suppose that they can be phases of any substance, or anywhere in physical space, at all.

8. Sensing and Knowing

It appears, then, that in order to " get outside the circle of our minds " it is not necessary for us to maintain that our awareness of sense-data is a kind of knowing. And indeed, if it is essential to knowledge that the object known should exist independently of the knowing of it, I have implicitly denied that our awareness of sense-data is a kind of knowing, for I have made it a necessary and sufficient condition of the existence of sense-data that they should in fact be experienced. But I am not sure that this is essential to knowledge, as it is ordinarily understood. The difficulty here is that the expression " object of knowledge " is ambiguous. It is used with reference both to our knowledge of the truth of propositions, and to our acquaintance with particular things. If we are concerned with propositional knowledge, then there is justification for saying that knowledge presupposes the independence of its object ; for it is essential to knowledge of this kind that the truth of the proposition known should not depend upon our knowing it. But it does not follow from this that the existence of a thing which we know, in the sense of being acquainted with it, must also be independent of our knowing it. Furthermore, this second sense of " knowledge " is itself ambiguous. For we tend to speak indifferently of being acquainted both with sense-data and with material things ; but if the term " acquaintance " is taken, as it usually is, to be equivalent to " direct awareness ", then in the sense in which it is applicable to sense-data, it is not applicable to material things. Accordingly, whether or not there is historical justification for speaking of knowing sense-data, it seems advisable for the sake of clarity not to use the word " knowledge " in this sense. To avoid ambiguity, I shall in future use the word " awareness " only in connexion with sense-data, and the word " perception " only in connexion with material things, and I shall restrict the use of the word " knowledge " to its propositional sense.

If one uses the word " knowledge " in this way, one cannot say that the awareness of sense-data is itself a kind of knowing ; but we will still have to say that it involves knowledge. For the meaning of the expression " direct awareness " is such that, whenever we are directly aware of a sense-datum, it follows that we know some proposition which describes the sense-datum to be true. But what is the character of this knowledge ? In the ordinary way, I think that all that is required for an empirical proposition to be known is that it should in fact be true, that no doubt should be felt about its truth, and that the belief in it should not have been reached by way of a belief in any false proposition, and should have good inductive grounds ; and in this sense we can claim to know propositions about the existence and properties of material things, and even general propositions, although our perceptions can never afford us a logical guarantee of their truth. But it is widely held that when we speak of knowing a proposition which describes a presented sense-datum, we imply more than this. It is held that we imply, not merely that our belief in the truth of such proposition is not, in fact, mistaken, but that it could not conceivably be mistaken. And it is this view that is sometimes expressed by the assertion that such propositions are " indubitable " or " incorrigible ".

But now it may be asked : How can any empirical proposition be indubitable in this sense ? We say that an *a priori* proposition is indubitable because its contradictory is self-contradictory, but this cannot be the ground for asserting that propositions describing presented sense-data are indubitable ; for it is not maintained that these propositions are analytic. But what other ground can there be for such an assertion ? It is not as if it meant only that we were psychologically unable to doubt these propositions ; for that might be true also of propositions about the existence of material things, which are supposed to be distinguished from propositions about the existence of sense-data partly by the fact that they are not indubitable in the sense that is here in question. It means rather that to doubt the truth of a proposition which describes a presented sense-datum is logically incorrect. But surely this is a condition that no empirical proposition can possibly satisfy ?

To see how this objection may be met, let me try to give an instance of the expression of an " incorrigible " proposition. Suppose that I experience a visual sense-datum which I describe by saying " this is green ", and suppose that I am using the sentence merely to designate the sense-datum in question, and am not implying that it is in any way related to anything that I am not simultaneously experiencing. Is there then any possibility of my being mistaken ? The answer is that I can at least be making a verbal mistake. It may, for instance, be a rule of the language I am supposed to be using that the correct name for the colour of such a sense-datum is " red " and not " green ". And if this is so I am, in a sense, misdescribing what I experience. But my mistake is not a mistake of the same kind as that

which I should be making if I took the sense-datum
to belong to the wrong material thing, or made any
other judgement that involved relating the sense-
datum falsely to further actual or possible experiences. Suppose, for example, that I had said " this
is a green book " and that there was really no book
there, or that the colour of the book was not really
green. In that case, I should have made not merely
a verbal error but an error of fact ; for I should
implicitly have asserted a number of hypothetical
propositions which, as I might subsequently discover, were not true ; I might find, for instance, that
when I went to open the supposed book it appeared
hollow inside, or that when I observed it in a clear
light it never again looked green. But whether or
not I actually discover that I am mistaken is not, for
the purpose of this illustration, of any importance.
What is important is that the possibility of my being
mistaken, in what is not merely a verbal sense,
depends upon the fact that my judgement goes
beyond the evidence upon which it is immediately
based. It connects an experienced sense-datum with
other possible sense-data which are not simultaneously given, and in doing so it allows room for
doubt and error. For it cannot be formally deduced
from a mere description of the immediate evidence
that these further sense-data would, in fact, be
obtainable even if the relevant conditions were fulfilled. In other words, the reason why I can be
making an error of fact in asserting a proposition of
this kind is that the proposition is not completely

verified by the existence of the sense-datum upon the observation of which it is based ; nor can it ever be completely verified. Consequently, although it may be irrational on the evidence to express doubt in its truth, it is always significant. But it is held to be characteristic of an " incorrigible " proposition that it is completely verified by the existence of the sense-datum which it describes ; and so it is inferred that to doubt the truth of such a proposition is not merely irrational but meaningless ; for it is only significant to doubt where there is a logical possibility of error. The argument is, in short, that if one uses a sentence such as " this is green " merely to designate a present sense-datum, then no proposition is being asserted to the truth of which any further evidence would be relevant. And from this it is concluded that all that one can properly mean in such a case by saying that one doubts whether this is green is that one is doubting whether " green " is the correct word to use. And the same would apply to any other sentence that was used only to designate some feature of what was actually being experienced, without being intended to carry any further implication. The propositions which such sentences were supposed to express might be said to be indubitable on the ground that it was not significant to say that one doubted them in any other but a purely verbal sense.

From this it may be concluded that all that is involved in the claim that there are indubitable or incorrigible empirical propositions is that people do sometimes use sentences in the way that the sentence

" this is green " was used in my example, or at any
rate that they could use certain sentences in this way,
if they chose. And I do not see any reason to deny
that this is so. It is indeed to be remarked that what
I have been calling verbal doubt is also, in a sense,
factual; for it is, after all, a question of fact whether
one's use of a word on a given occasion is or is not
in accordance with one's own habitual usage, or with
the usage of other people. But the point is that
whereas, in the case of most empirical propositions,
it would still be possible to doubt them even if there
were no doubt that the relevant words were being
correctly used, this possibility does not extend to the
class of propositions about sense-data that I have
been considering. And the reason for this is simply
the linguistic fact that we do not attach any meaning
to the statement that we doubt these propositions, in
this further non-verbal sense of " doubting " in
which we do attach meaning to the statement that
we doubt the others.

9. The Errors of Formalism

A curious fact about this question of incorrigible
propositions is that the answers which philosophers
have given to it have usually been made to depend
upon the view they have taken of what, at first
sight, appears to be an entirely different problem.
For, on the one hand, it has been assumed by those
who maintain that some empirical propositions must
be incorrigible that their case would be proved if

they could show that the truth or falsity of empirical propositions depended in the last resort, not upon relations that they bore to one another, but upon their accordance or discordance with observable facts ; so that the main arguments which these philosophers have produced in favour of there being incorrigible propositions have been arguments against the coherence theory of truth.   And, conversely, what those who have rejected the view that there can be incorrigible propositions appear, for the most part, to have been mainly anxious to deny is that any propositions do, or can, refer to facts, unless this is interpreted as being merely a misleading way of saying that they have certain relations to other propositions.   In dealing with this point, the course that I shall follow is to consider first the problem of the relationship of propositions to facts, and then to see what bearing, if any, the solution of this problem has on the question whether any empirical propositions are incorrigible.

The position of those who deny the possibility of expressing propositions that refer to empirical facts, in the sense in which " reference to a fact " is ordinarily understood, may be summarized as follows. They hold that all that is necessary for the specification of a language is an account of what Professor Carnap has called its formation and transformation rules.   The formation rules determine what combinations of signs are to constitute proper sentences of the language ; the transformation rules prescribe the ways in which these sentences may legitimately

D

be derived from one another. Both these sets of rules are held to be purely formal in character ; and this means that they contain " no reference to the meaning of the symbols (for example, the words) or to the sense of the expressions (*e.g.* the sentences), but simply and solely to the kinds and order of the symbols from which the expressions are constructed ".[1] Consequently, if a distinction is made between the sentences that express *a priori* and those that express empirical propositions, it can be only in virtue of a difference in the form of the symbols which they contain, or in the nature of the formal relations which they have to other sentences. In the case of languages which allow the expression of empirical propositions, it is thought possible to mark out a special class of sentences, which are referred to as " observation " or " protocol " or " basic " sentences ; and it is held to be a necessary and sufficient condition of the admissibility of any sentence that is intended to express an empirical proposition that some observation-sentence should be derivable from it in accordance with the established rules of the language. One must not, however, be misled by the name of these observation-sentences into supposing that they refer to observable facts ; or that the test which they provide for the validity of empirical propositions is one of correspondence with fact, as this is ordinarily understood. For the properties by which these sentences are essentially distinguished are intended to be purely formal ; and

[1] Rudolf Carnap, *The Logical Syntax of Language*, p. 1.

the only criterion that is allowed for determining the truth or falsity of any " observation-statement " is the formal possibility of incorporating it in a given system. Nor does this criterion give them any advantage over statements of other kinds. For it is held that even when a hypothesis " proves to be logically incompatible with certain protocol-sentences, there always exists the possibility of maintaining the hypothesis and renouncing acknowledgement of the protocol-sentences ".[1] All that is required is that the system of propositions which is accepted as true should be formally self-consistent. And this is supposed to be the sole criterion of their truth.

I do not think that any very elaborate argument is needed to show that this theory is altogether untenable. In the first place, it is not true that we are able to use or understand a language when we are acquainted only with its formation and trans-formation rules. These rules are indeed sufficient for the characterization of a purely abstract system of logic or mathematics, so long as no attempt is made to give the system a material interpretation ; but they are not sufficient for the characterization of any language that serves to communicate proposi-tions about matters of fact. From the transforma-tion rules we can learn that in any situation in which we are entitled to use a given sentence of the language, we are also entitled to use certain others ; but neither they nor the formation rules afford us any means of knowing what are the situations in which

[1] *Ibid.* p. 318.

any single sentence can legitimately be used. But until this is determined the " language " in question is not, in the ordinary sense, a language at all. For it does not serve to communicate anything. It is merely a formal calculus which we do not know how to apply. For it to become a language it is necessary that some at least of the expressions that it contains should be given a meaning. And this is effected by the method of ostensive definition, that is, by correlating these expressions, not with other expressions, but with what is actually observed. Professor Carnap has indeed asserted that these " so-called ostensive definitions " are themselves " translations of words ". According to him, to define, for example, an elephant, ostensively, is merely to lay down the transformation rule " ' elephant '=animal of the same kind as the animal in this or that position in space-time ".[1]   But this is clearly a mistake. It is true that if I teach someone the meaning of the English word " elephant " by pointing to a particular animal, the information he receives is that an elephant is an animal of the same kind as that which he is observing at a particular place and time. But this is not to say that the word " elephant " is synonymous in English with any such expression as " animal of the same kind as that which, on July 2nd, 1939, was standing 30 yards south-west of the bandstand at the London Zoo ". For even if it is a fact that an elephant was actually to be observed at that particular place and time, it is not

---

[1] *The Unity of Science*, p. 39.

a necessary fact. I may be expressing a false proposition if I say that there was no animal standing
30 yards south-west of the bandstand at the London
Zoo on July 2nd, 1939, or that there was such an
animal but it was not an elephant; but I shall
certainly not be contradicting myself. The spatio-
temporal description may serve to indicate the
context in which some word has been, or is being,
ostensively defined, but it is not in itself a substitute
for that context. And it is only by reference to an
empirical context that any ostensive definition is to
be understood.

Having allowed the possibility of ostensive definitions, we might then consider that we required a
special name for the class of sentences whose constituents were defined in this way; and it would
be reasonable for us to call them observation-
sentences, on the ground that they were intended to
refer to what could be directly observed. But this
cannot be what those who uphold the theory I am
now considering mean by an observation-sentence.
For, in effect, they deny the possibility of using any
sentence to refer to what can be directly observed.
As they use it, the term " observation-sentence " is
purely syntactical. The sentences to which it is
applied are distinguished from other sentences
merely by the fact that they contain different words
and obey different transformation rules. But what
is the point of this conventional distinction? It
seems to be intended to furnish a principle of
empiricism. The theory is that one excludes meta-

physics by asserting that every proposition that is not analytic must be " empirically testable " and by defining this " testability " in terms of the derivation of observation-sentences. But this use of the term " empirically testable " is again very misleading. For what sort of empirical test is provided by the fact that the conventional rules of a language allow one sentence to be formally derived from another, when neither sentence is to be understood as recording what can be actually experienced ? One does not become an empiricist merely by a free use of the word " empirical " or the word " observation ".

If we were to take this view of the nature of observation-sentences, it clearly would not matter whether we agreed with Carnap that " every concrete sentence belonging to the physicalistic system-language can in suitable circumstances serve as an observation-sentence ",[1] or whether we required that these sentences should have a special form. For it would only be a question of how we chose to apply a syntactical designation ; and in either case it would be an arbitrary choice. It has, indeed, been argued [2] that the form in which we choose to cast these sentences may make a difference to the " stability " of the propositions they express, in the sense that it may give them a greater or lesser chance of being retained in the accepted system of proposi-

---

[1] " Über Protokollsätze ", Erkenntnis, Band 3, p. 224.

[2] Cf. Otto Neurath, " Protokollsätze ", Erkenntnis, Band 3; and for criticism, my article on " Verification and Experience ", Proceedings of the Aristotelian Society, 1936–7, where I put forward a more detailed refutation of the whole of this version of the coherence theory of truth.

tions, and so of being " true " in the only sense in which the exponents of this theory recognize the notion of truth. But this must be a mistake. For if the only possible criterion of the truth of a proposition is its logical compatibility with other propositions, then it cannot be necessary to devise a special form for its expression in order to secure its retention in the accepted system. It is sufficient for us, if we wish to retain it, simply to decide to exclude all propositions that are inconsistent with it. This is admittedly an arbitrary procedure ; but so would be any other procedure that we could adopt. Provided that it is internally self-consistent we may, on this view, regard as " true " any system of propositions that we choose. And so long as the suggestion of an appeal to the observable facts is ruled out as meaningless, no question of justification can arise.

But suppose now, what is admitted to be possible, that we are confronted with two mutually exclusive sets of propositions, each of which is internally self-consistent. Are we to say that both are independently true ? If we do, we contradict ourselves, according to the meaning that we ordinarily give to " truth ". We must look therefore for some method of deciding between these incompatible systems. But what method can there be if the only criterion of the truth of any system is its internal self-consistency ? I believe that this objection is unanswerable. An attempt has indeed been made to answer it by saying that the true system is that which happens to be accepted by accredited observers, such as the scientists of our era.[1] But now we may ask whether the true system is merely that which contains in itself the proposition that it alone is accepted by these scientists, or whether it is that which is so accepted, as a matter of fact. In the former case the proposed criterion does not effect what is required of it. For each of several incompatible systems might contain the proposition that it alone was the accepted one, without being internally inconsistent. But to adopt the other alternative is to abandon the coherence theory of truth. For it involves, what the advocates of the theory hold to be impossible, a comparison of a proposition with the empirical facts. And if this comparison is allowed in the case of a proposition about the behaviour of contemporary scientists, why not in other cases also ? Is it not conceivable even that actual observation might show that contemporary scientists sometimes made mistakes ?

10. SENTENCES, PROPOSITIONS, AND FACTS

I hope that by now enough has been said to show that the consequences of denying the possibility of using words to refer to empirical facts are altogether unacceptable. But I have still to explain how this denial ever came to be made. One may infer that it is due to some confusion of thought, if the foregoing argument is correct. But what is the source of this confusion ? I suggest that it may be found

[1] Cf. Carnap, " Erwiderung auf die Aufsätze von E. Zilsel und K. Duncker ", *Erkenntnis*, Band 3, pp. 179-80 ; and Carl Hempel, " Some Remarks on Empiricism ", *Analysis*, vol. iii, No. 3.

in the formulation of the two illegitimate questions : How is it possible for symbols to have meaning ? and, What is it that they mean ? And I hope that in discussing these questions I shall be able to elucidate the meaning of such puzzling but indispensable expressions as " the reference of symbols to objects " or " the comparison of propositions with facts ".

I shall begin with the question, What does a symbol, for example a word, or a sentence, mean ? This is a question that we have no difficulty in answering, so long as it is taken to refer only to particular cases. If anyone does not understand the meaning of a particular sentence, or word, there are various ways of enlightening him. One method is that of translation into another language, or into an equivalent expression of the same language, as when it is said that " I am thirsty " means " J'ai soif ", or that " nephew " means " brother's or sister's son ". In such cases it is assumed that the explanatory symbols are already understood by the person for whose benefit the translation is made. Another method is that of giving examples to indicate the kind of situation to which a symbol may legitimately be applied. Thus, if I wish to explain to someone the meaning of " jealousy ", instead of attempting to produce an explicit verbal definition, I may give him some description of the way in which jealous people behave. I may, for example, refer him to Shakespeare's tragedy of *Othello* or to Proust's *Du Côté de chez Swann*. To this it may be objected that it is possible to be jealous without behaving exactly like either Othello or Swann, and that what is wanted is a description of the necessary and sufficient conditions of jealousy, which would be tantamount to giving an explicit definition of the word. But the fact is that the word " jealousy ", like many others, is used with too little precision, for it to be possible to indicate any single set of circumstances the occurrence of which is both necessary and sufficient for its proper application. It is applied to a relatively indefinite range of situations ; and it is for this reason that the method of giving examples is appropriate for making its meaning understood. Finally, there is the method of ostensive definition, which we employ when we indicate the meaning of a symbol by correlating it with some perceived object or event ; and this differs from the other methods in that it does not, to be effective, require any previous understanding of the meaning of other symbols. It is tempting to think that this method is logically indispensable, which I take to have been the view of those empiricists who denied the possibility of " innate ideas ". But this is not so. For it is logically conceivable that people should use words correctly and understand their meaning without any process of learning at all. What is necessary, as we have seen, is that a language should contain non-formal rules of meaning ; but we must not confuse the employment of these rules with the process of learning them. We have, however, good reason to suppose that the correct use of symbols has, in fact, to be learned. And so we may say that it is at least causally requisite that the meaning of some expressions should be explained ostensively, if any are to be understood.

I have now given a description of the ways in which one may explain the meaning of any given symbol. But, paradoxically, this does not enable one to answer the general question : What do symbols mean ? For the fact is that those who ask this question do not require the kind of information that such explanations give. Their problem is not that they fail to understand any symbols. It is of an entirely different character. It arises out of the assumption that " meaning " is a relation which a symbol bears to something. And the puzzle is to discover the nature of this other term.

If we take this puzzle seriously, our first inclination may be to try to solve it without postulating anything beyond what we experience. The meaning of a sentence, we may say, is an empirical fact. And we may explain that we give the name of " empirical fact " to whatever can be actually observed. If we say this, we shall have, presumably, to draw a distinction between those sentences that signify directly and those that signify indirectly, and to define the meaning of the sentences of this second class in terms of the meaning of the observation-sentences to which, as we must argue, they are capable of being reduced ; and here already there are serious difficulties. But even if we suppose these difficulties to be overcome, and at the same time set aside the problem of the sentences that are ordinarily held to express *a priori* propositions, by saying either that they too are empirical, or else, more plausibly, that they are not meaningful in the same sense as the others, our theory will still be untenable. And to see that this is so, we have only to reflect that some sentences are used to express what is empirically false. Now there is no question but that these sentences are meaningful. But what they mean cannot be empirical facts; for, in this case, there are no such facts. Moreover, it is clear that the meaning of a sentence is independent of the truth or falsity of what it is used to express. If, for example, I say that there is a stove in my room and there is actually no stove in my room, I am expressing a falsehood; if there is a stove, I am expressing a truth; but the meaning of my sentence remains the same, whether or not there is actually a stove in my room. But if the meaning of a sentence is the same, whether what it expresses is true or false, and if in the case where it expresses a falsehood it cannot mean an empirical fact, then it does not mean an empirical fact even when it happens to express what is true. And so we must look for some other answer to the question, What do sentences mean?

The course that is favoured by most philosophers who have paid attention to this question is to invent a class of would-be facts, which they call " propositions ". By doing this they are able to provide a verbal solution for the problem that I am discussing; but the solution is no more than verbal. We are told that what a sentence means is a proposition ; but if we then ask what a proposition is, the only definition available is that it is what a sentence means. These propositions are, admittedly, not capable of being observed ; nevertheless it is sometimes held that they are objectively real, even though they do not exist in the way that natural objects exist. But no criterion is given by means of which one could decide when a thing was to be accounted " real ", in this non-empirical sense. It is not surprising, therefore, that philosophers who regard themselves as empiricists should find themselves unable to attach any significance to this notion of real propositions ; and so they come to see no alternative but to try to define the meaning of symbols exclusively in terms of their relations to other symbols. And thus they fall into the errors of formalism, which I have already exposed.

I shall not cast about for further answers to the question, What do symbols mean ? For the view that I am taking is that the reason why this problem appears to defy solution is that there is really no problem to solve. We cannot find " the other term of the relation of meaning ", because the assumption that meaning is a relation which somehow unites a symbol with some other unspecified object is itself erroneous. What one is asking for when one seeks to know the meaning of a symbol is an explanation of the way in which the symbol is used. What form such explanations may take in particular cases I have already shown. But I cannot deal in the same

way with the general case, for the simple reason that
there is no general usage to explain. There is no
one thing that all symbols mean. Accordingly, if
one is asked what is the meaning of a sentence or a
word, one must counter with the questions : What
sentence ? What word ? Then, if instances are
given, one may be able to explain what they mean.
But until the question is made definite in this way
it cannot possibly be answered. It is indeed conceivable that there should be a language of such
poverty that every one of its expressions was equivalent to every other ; and then if one were asked
what the sentences of this language meant, one
would be able to answer, either demonstratively, or
else by setting forth a sentence of some other
language, which was a translation of them all. But
this condition is not satisfied by any language that
anybody has ever used. Thus, I can explain the
meaning of any given sentence in English by one
of the methods that I have described. But I cannot
explain what English sentences mean, in general.
For their meanings do not happen all to be the same.

Analogous to the question, What do symbols
mean ? is the question, What are the objects of the
various activities of our understandings ? What is
it that we know, or doubt, or suppose, or imagine,
or wonder, or believe ? It may be thought that one
can dispose of the case of knowledge by saying that
it is always facts that are known ; but this answer
is not available for the other cases. For it is admitted
that one can believe, and *a fortiori* suppose or imagine

or doubt, what is actually false. Here again, recourse
is had to the notion of a proposition ; and here again
the solution is purely verbal. For a proposition, in
this usage, is itself defined as the object of these
intellective acts. But the fact is that " believing ",
" imagining " and the rest, resemble " meaning " in
that they are not relations, like " loving " or " killing ", that require any real object at all. The only
way in which I can answer the question, What is it
that you doubt, or wonder, or believe ? is by giving
actual examples. " I doubt whether all physical
phenomena can be explained in terms of the field
theory " ; " I wonder whether Sir Philip Francis
really was the author of the Junius letters " ; " I
believe that the introduction of the mandatory
system has been beneficial to the natives in Africa ".
But so long as the question is left indefinite, it cannot
be answered. There is no one thing that people
believe, any more than there is one thing that all
symbols mean. And the same, it may be added, is
true of knowledge. To say that the objects of knowledge are facts is no more illuminating than to say
that the objects of belief are propositions, except in
so far as it indicates that we do not speak of knowing
what is not actually true. For the sense of " knowledge " which is here in question is not that of
" acquaintance " or " awareness ", but that in which
we speak of knowing that something is the case.
Consequently, the word " fact " cannot, in this usage,
be regarded as a name for what can actually be
observed, but only as the equivalent of " true

proposition ". And it would therefore be less misleading if we said outright that it was always a proposition that was known. But the truth is that
" knowing ", in this sense, is not, any more than
" believing ", a relation that requires any real object.
If I am asked what do I know, I again can do no more
than give instances. " I know that light travels with
a velocity of approximately 186,000 miles a second."
" I know that 7 is a prime number." " I know that
vultures are carnivorous." Having given such
instances, I can then go on to classify them. I may,
for example, distinguish what belongs to mathematics from what belongs to physics, or what is
general from what is particular, or what is necessary
from what is contingent. And the fact that such
classifications are possible may be taken to show that
some instances of knowledge have something more in
common than what is needed merely to constitute
them instances of knowledge. But this does not
justify the view that all instances of knowledge have a
common feature of this kind. The fact that we are
able to give a name to the " common object " of all
acts or states of knowledge is not to the purpose.
For to say that people always know, or believe,
propositions is no more informative than to say that
they love their beloveds, or hunt quarry, or eat food.
It tells us no more than that we believe what we
believe, and know what we know.

It must not be inferred from this that I wish to
condemn the use of the word " proposition " altogether. Indeed, it will have been observed that I

have constantly used it myself. And it is necessary
to have such a word in order that one may be able to
refer to the meaning of sentences without having to
specify them particularly. Its use may be illustrated
by such an example as " In the course of his speech
he asserted a number of propositions of which I can
now remember nothing except that at least three of
them were false ". This cannot be translated by an
expression which contains a clause of the form " he
said '*a*' and '*b*' and '*c*', and not *a* and not *b* and not *c*",
where "*a*", "*b*" and "*c*" are designations of particular
indicative sentences. For it is possible that he did not
say "*a*", "*b*" and "*c*", but made some other statements,
"*d*," "*e*" and "*f*", which were false; and even if he did
in fact say "*a*", "*b*" and "*c*", and it is false that *a* or *b* or
c, it is still consistent with the truth of " he asserted at
least three false propositions ", that these statements
should not have been the ones in question. This
case is analogous to that of expressions like " someone has left his gloves in my room ", which is not
equivalent to " Smith has left his gloves in my room",
even though it was in fact Smith who did leave them.
For it is equally consistent with the truth of " someone has left his gloves in my room " that it should
not have been Smith, but Jones or Robinson or
someone else. Nor can the word " someone " be
replaced by a disjunction of names, or descriptions,
of particular persons. For the number of possible
candidates is infinite. And, for the same reason, it
is not possible, in cases where the word " proposition " is used in this indefinite way, to replace it by

means of a disjunction of names, or descriptions, of particular sentences. But is not the indefinite word " sentence " itself sufficient for this usage ? Why do we require to speak of propositions as well ? The answer is that we often wish to make statements which apply not merely to a given indicative sentence, but also to any other sentence, whether of the same or of a different language, that has the same meaning ; and our use of the word " proposition " enables us to do this concisely. Thus, to take a simple instance, if I say that the proposition " this is red " entails " this is not green ", I am not saying merely that the English sentence " this is not green " can legitimately be derived from " this is red " ; for my assertion could equally well be understood in terms of some other language, such as German or French. It applies not only to these particular English sentences but to any sentences, in any language, that are equivalent to them. And it is this that the use of the word " proposition " conveys. In general, we use the word " proposition " rather than " sentence " whenever we are concerned, not with the precise form of an expression, or the fact that it belongs to a particular language, but with its meaning. Consequently, we speak of propositions, and not sentences, as being true or false.

In this way we arrive also at the use of the word " proposition " to stand for the " object " of an intellection. For only that which is true can be known ; and only that which is capable of being true or false can be supposed, or doubted, or

imagined, or believed. Here again, we require a word
for the purpose of indirect reference. For example, if
I say that my friend believes whatever he reads in his
newspaper, I am not thereby saying " my friend believes that p, or my friend believes that q ", where
"p" and "q" are designations of particular sentences,
even if it happens to be the case that his newspaper
does in fact contain the sentences "p" and "q"; for it
is consistent with the truth of his believing whatever he reads in his newspaper that "p" and "q"
should not be among the sentences that it contains.
Or again, if I say " he has forgotten more than I
shall ever know ", I am not specifying precisely what
it is that he has forgotten and I shall never know.
No doubt if one were determined not to use any
word in the way in which the word " proposition "
is used, one could always find some other form of
expression. In the examples that I have just given,
I have avoided it by the use of indefinite relative
clauses. But this course is not always feasible. It
will not serve us in the case of such an example as
" he asserted two propositions, which you probably
believe but I doubt ". This might perhaps be translated into " two of his assertions are probable beliefs
of yours, but doubts of mine ", but I think it would
be generally admitted that this was not a felicitous
expression, and that the use of the word " proposition " was more convenient. Nor need it give rise
to any philosophical perplexity so long as we remember in using it that " meaning ", " knowing ",
" believing " and the rest are not relations, like

" loving " or " killing ", that require a real object,
and that to say that people know, or believe or doubt
propositions, or that a proposition is what a sentence
means, is, at best, to explain the use of the word
" proposition ", and is not to make a statement of
fact.

With this I complete my discussion of the
question, What do symbols mean ? The question,
How is it possible for symbols to mean ? may be
dealt with more shortly, for it is a product of the
same confusion as the other. Again, it is assumed
that meaning is a relation, analogous to loving or
killing ; but this time the puzzle is not to find the
other term of the relation, but to discover the nature
of the relation itself. What must be the connexion,
it is asked, between the word " cats ", for example,
and cats, or between the sentence " this is a pencil "
and the fact that this is a pencil, for one to be able to
symbolize the other ? Sometimes the answer given
is that the relation is causal. " What do we know
when we know that our words ' express ' something
we see ? I see a cat and say ' there is a cat '. Someone also says ' Why did you say " there is a cat " ? '
and I reply, ' because I saw a cat '. The word
' because ' must be taken as expressing a relation
which is, at least partly, that of cause and effect." [1]
Another answer is that the relation is one of structural
identity. " The sentence is a picture of reality. In
the picture and the pictured there must be something

---

[1] Bertrand Russell, " The Limits of Empiricism ", *Proceedings
of the Aristotelian Society*, 1935-6.

identical in order that the one can be a picture of
the other at all.   What the picture must have in
common with reality in order to be able to represent
it after its manner — rightly or falsely — is the form
of representation.   To the configuration of the
simple signs in the sentential sign corresponds the
configuration of the objects in the state of affairs.
In the sentence there must be exactly as many things
distinguishable as there are in the state of affairs
which it represents." [1]   Now it is not to be denied
that the utterance of a symbol is very often caused
by a perception of that which it symbolizes ; and
it is true also that there are some symbols that do
have the same structure as the states of affairs which
they represent.   But it cannot rightly be inferred
that the essence of meaning consists in either of
these relations, if only for the reason that a symbol
may legitimately be used to express what is false.[2]
We cannot define the meaning of a symbol in terms
of any relation that is supposed to hold between it
and the fact which it symbolizes, for in cases where
it expresses a falsehood there is no such fact, and
consequently no such relation ; and yet the symbol
is still meaningful.   Moreover, even when a symbol
does symbolize what is actually observed, it is not

---

[1] Ludwig Wittgenstein, *Tractatus Logico-Philosophicus*, Propositions 4.01, 2.161, 2.17, 3.21, 4.04.   I have translated " Satz "
by " sentence " instead of " proposition ", which appears in the
English version given in the book.

[2] Cf. R. B. Braithwaite, " The Relation of Psychology to
Logic ", *Supplementary Proceedings of the Aristotelian Society*,
1938 ; and my own article " On the Scope of Empirical Knowledge ", *Erkenntnis*, Band 7, Heft 4.

necessary that its utterance should be caused by a perception of that which is symbolized, or that it should bear any resemblance to it, whether in structure or content. It does not follow from the fact that I assert that I am seeing a cat at a time when I actually am seeing a cat that my utterance is the effect of this perception. I may, for example, have been hypnotically induced to make such a statement at that particular time. And while the symbol that I use may take the form of a picture or a model, it certainly need not. Given suitable conventions, I can express the fact that I am seeing a cat by representing it pictorially; and there may be circumstances in which the choice of such a method of representation has practical advantages. For instance, if I wish to express some facts of geography, I may find it most convenient to do so by means of a map. But even if this method were universally applicable, and invariably advantageous, which in fact it is not, it still would not have any logical pre-eminence. There is no reason whatever for supposing that all the sentences of the English or any other European language are really, in any ordinary sense, pictures or models of what they represent. But this does not in the least prevent them from being meaningful.

The adherents of the formalist theory of language have seen that a symbol need not be connected with what it symbolizes, either causally, or by having the same structure, or indeed by any other natural relation. But they have mistakenly gone on to infer that the only rules of meaning that can be admitted in the characterization of a language are the formal rules by which one symbol is connected with another. Against this, I have already shown that if a " language " is to be capable of being used as a language, that is to say, for the purpose of communication, it must also be characterized by non-formal rules, which connect some of its symbols, not with other symbols, but with observable states of affairs. What is not necessary, however, is that a symbol, the use of which is determined by such a non-formal rule, should have any further connexion with what it symbolizes beyond that which is constituted by the existence of the rule. The answer to the question, How is it possible for " red " to mean red ? is simply that this happens to be the symbol that we have chosen to use to refer to this colour. The spoken word " red " differs from words like " whistle " or " hiss " in that it does not in the least resemble that which it is used to symbolize ; but this fact does not furnish any logical objection to our using it in the way that we do. A symbol may or may not share a common quality with that which it symbolizes. There is no ground whatsoever for saying that it must.

I believe that this mistake about the nature of meaning is reflected in the ordinary formulation of " the correspondence theory of truth ". For when we are told that a sentence expresses a true proposition if and only if it is used in such a way that it corresponds to a fact, we are inclined to interpret the word " correspondence " literally, as implying some sort of resemblance, and then we find ourselves confronted with such questions as, What do sentences which express false propositions resemble? and How is it that sentences, which express what we have every reason for supposing to be true propositions, do not appear in any way to resemble the relevant facts? — and to these questions we are unable to give any satisfactory answer. But such problems do not arise, once it is made clear that the word " correspondence ", if it is to be used at all in this connexion, must not be understood literally. To say that I am using the sentence " there is a match-box on my table " to correspond to the fact that there is a match-box on my table, or to express a proposition which corresponds to this fact, is to say no more than that I am using the words " there is a match-box on my table " to mean that there is a match-box on my table, and there is a match-box on my table. But how do I discover that there is a match-box on my table? How is it to be determined that any empirical proposition does, in this sense, correspond to a fact? The answer is that, in the last resort, it is always to be determined by actual observation. I say " in the last resort " because it is necessary here to draw a distinction between propositions the truth of which is determined directly by observation, and those that are verified indirectly. One's ground for believing a given proposition is often, in the first instance, the truth of a second proposition which is evidence for it; and one's ground for believing the second proposition may, in its turn, be the truth of

a third ; but this series cannot be prolonged indefinitely. In the end it must include at least one
proposition that is believed, not merely on the
ground that it is supported by other propositions,
but in virtue of what is actually observed. For, as
I have already shown, we are not entitled to regard
a set of propositions as true merely because they support one another. In order that we should have
reason to accept any of them, it is necessary that at
least one of their number should be directly verified
by observation of an empirical fact.

Is it now possible for us to delimit the class of
propositions that are capable of being directly
verified ? The only means that I can see of doing
this is to say that a proposition is capable of being
directly verified when it is expressed by a sentence
the meaning of which is determined by a non-formal
rule. But the consequence of this is that the question,
whether a given proposition is or is not capable of
being directly verified, does not admit of a straightforward answer. We must say that it depends upon
the language in which the proposition is expressed.
If, for example, we have agreed to use the sense-
datum language, we shall have to say that propositions like " this is a match-box " or " this is a
pencil " are not directly verifiable.[1] For we must
hold that the meaning of sentences which express such
propositions is to be determined by reference to

---

[1] This must not be understood to imply that the validity of
such propositions consists in anything other than the occurrence
of the relevant sense-data. Cf. section 22 of this book.

sentences which designate sense-data, and that it is only when a sentence explicitly designates a sense-data that its meaning is determined by reference to fact. On the other hand, when we are teaching English to a child, we imply that propositions about material things can be directly verified. For we do not then explain the meaning of sentences like " this is a match-box " or " this is a pencil " in terms of sentences which designate sense-data. We indicate it ostensively. But whereas the meaning of a sentence which refers to a sense-datum is precisely determined by the rule that correlates it with the sense-datum in question, such precision is not attainable in the case of a sentence which refers to a material thing. For the proposition which such a sentence expresses differs from a proposition about a sense-datum in that there are no observable facts that constitute both a necessary and sufficient condition of its truth. We may indicate the meaning of a sentence of this type by giving a sample of the kind of evidence that directly supports the truth of the proposition it expresses, but we do not intend to suggest that this evidence is exhaustive. Suppose, for example, that I teach someone the meaning of the sentence " this is a match-box " by actually showing him a match-box, opening it, taking out and striking a match, and so forth. If, subsequently, he says " this is a match-box ", and there is in fact no match-box there, it does not follow that he has failed to apprehend the rule that I tried to teach him. His error may be, not that he has mistaken the meaning of the sentence he is using, but that, having acquired some evidence in favour of the proposition which it expresses, he has wrongly assumed the possibility of increasing the sum of this favourable evidence indefinitely. If he then experiments further and finds the new evidence unfavourable, he may admit that when he used the sentence " this is a match-box " he was expressing a false proposition ; but this does not mean that he was not justified in using it, in view of the evidence which he had. To be deceived by one's senses is not necessarily to be mistaken about the meaning of words.

My conclusion is, then, that we can have no reason to believe in the truth of any set of empirical propositions unless at least one of them can be directly verified ; and that, for a proposition to be directly verifiable, it is necessary that the meaning of the sentence which expresses it should be determined by correlation with some observable state of affairs, though this correlation need not be univocal. Where the correlation is univocal, as in the case of a sentence which refers to a sense-datum, it is possible to be mistaken about the truth of the proposition expressed, so long as one is not actually observing the relevant fact. But there is no such possibility of error when the sense-datum in question is actually being sensed. For in that case the use of the sentence is prescribed by a rule of the language ; so that to make an assertion that does not correspond to the fact is either to tell a deliberate lie or else to make a verbal mistake. It is for this reason that philosophers have held, as we have seen, that sentences of this kind express " incorrigible " propositions ; and so, since any process of verification can be described in terms of the sense-datum language, they have inferred that unless it is possible for some empirical propositions to be " incorrigible ", there can be no ground for supposing any empirical proposition to be true. And if they are willing to define an " incorrigible " proposition as one that is expressed by a sentence the denial of which is a contravention of a non-formal rule of meaning, their conclusion is correct. For it is then a way of saying that if we are to be able to express any proposition that is capable of being verified, it is necessary that, besides the rules which correlate symbols with other symbols, our language should also contain rules of meaning, which correlate symbols with observable facts. It implies that we cannot, as I have shown, obtain a satisfactory criterion of truth merely by setting up a formal calculus for deriving sentences from one another, and then paying lip-service to empiricism by calling some of them observation-sentences. Accordingly, if one is to maintain the principle that no sentence can be said to express an empirical proposition unless some observation-sentence is derivable from it, it must be made clear that the truth of the propositions that are expressed by these observation-sentences is determined, not by merely formal criteria, but by the fact that they correspond directly, in the sense I have indicated, to what can be observed.

11. THE NATURE OF THE " GIVEN "

It follows from what I have said that the questions
which Professor Carnap classifies as "problems of the
so-called given or primitive data " [1] do not, as he
maintains, fall entirely within the scope of logical
syntax. His view is that the question " What objects
are the elements of given, direct experience ? " is
really verbal. He thinks that it is equivalent to
asking " What kinds of word occur in observation-
sentences ? ", and that the answer to this question
depends wholly upon one's choice of language.
Consequently, he holds that it may be decided by
convention whether " the elements that are directly
given are the simplest sensations and feelings ", or
whether they are " more complex objects, such as
partial *gestalts* of single sensory fields " ; for, according to him, these are not alternative theses about an
empirical matter of fact, but alternative suggestions
about the forms of observation-sentences, and it is
open to us to give our observation-sentences any
form that we please.[2] But this reasoning is fallacious.
The choice of the language of sense-data to describe
what we observe, rather than the language of appearing, or the language of multiple location, is indeed
conventional ; and it is a matter of convention that
in referring to sense-data we should use the particular
signs that we do. But it does not follow from this
that the propositions which are intended to describe

[1] *The Logical Syntax of Language*, pp. 305-6.
[2] *The Unity of Science*, pp. 45-7.

the characteristics of sense-data are true only by convention. For sense-data can have properties other than those that belong to them by definition; and to describe these properties is not to express a rule of language, but to make a statement of fact. It is true that, so long as it is framed in purely general terms, the question, What do people observe? does admit only of a verbal answer. For there is no one common quality that is shared by everything that is observed. But this does not prove that sense-data cannot be brought under any empirical classifications, or that the question, What do people observe? cannot be answered factually when it is understood to refer to particular cases. In this respect it may be compared with the question, What do people eat? If we answer this by saying that people eat food, we are treating it merely as a verbal question; for if we are asked what we mean by the word "food", we have to reply that we use it to refer to whatever people eat. But it does not follow from this that the subject of food cannot be treated as an empirical science. We should think a philosopher very silly who maintained that all problems about nutrition were purely verbal, on the ground that they could be reformulated as questions about the words that occurred in nutrition-sentences. But his argument would be exactly on a level with that which Carnap uses to dispose of the "problems of the so-called given". Such questions as whether the *gestalt* or the atomic theory more adequately describes the nature of our visual sense-fields must be decided, not by a verbal convention, but by an examination of the empirical evidence.

The analogy on which I have just drawn has been used also by Professor Prichard. " Grant ", he says, " for the sake of argument that on some occasion I am apprehending in the form of perceiving a particular sound, a particular colour, and a particular feeling of roughness. Then, no doubt, any one of them is being thus apprehended by me. Nevertheless it is not *a* something which is being thus apprehended. If I am eating a number of things, say, some cheese, some bread, and some salt, they together form a certain numerical group, viz. the totality of things which I am eating. But their membership of this group does not constitute them things having a certain common character. . . . The things which I am eating are united simply by my eating them ; and my eating them does not constitute them things of a certain sort. Indeed to speak of *a* something which is being eaten by me, or of something which is being eaten by someone is merely verbal, because to be being eaten is not a character of anything. Similarly the colour, the sound and the feeling of roughness which I am thus apprehending are united solely by my thus apprehending them ; and though each is one of the things which are being thus apprehended by me, none is *a* something which is being thus apprehended by me. There is no such thing as a thing which is being thus apprehended by me, nor again such a thing as a thing which is being thus apprehended by someone." [1] The argument is not very clearly stated ; but I take it that Prichard is maintaining that what we may call the relational property of " being apprehended " resembles the relational property of " being eaten " in that the possession of it does not logically entail the possession of any special quality ; and with this I am prepared to agree. And if in saying that " to speak of *a* something which is being eaten by someone is purely verbal " he means that the proposition " people eat food " is analytic, I agree with this also ; and I agree that the same applies to the proposition that people apprehend sense-data. But it does not follow, as Prichard seems to think, that " there could not be such a thing as a sense-datum ", any more than it follows that there could not be such a thing as food. As I use the word " sense-datum ", to deny that there were sense-data would be to deny that anything ever was observed ; and I cannot believe that Professor Prichard, or any other philosopher, really wishes to deny this. Admittedly, the facts which one seeks to describe by referring to sense-data could also be described in some other terminology. But a proposition does not cease to be true merely because there is more than one way of expressing it.

It should by now be clear that in saying that there are sense-data I am not either assuming or rejecting any special empirical theory about the nature of

[1] " The Sense-datum Fallacy ", *Supplementary Proceedings of the Aristotelian Society*, 1938, pp. 14-15.

what we observe. Nor do I wish to defend all that the advocates of sense-data have said of them ; for I have already pointed out that their use of the term has not always been clear or even consistent. One source of confusion to which I have referred is the inclination to treat sense-data as if they were a species of material things. Another with which I must now deal is the use of a physical rather than a psychological criterion to determine what it is that we directly observe. This leads on some occasions to the view that more is given to us than we are actually aware of ; on other occasions, to the view that only a part of what we apprehend is " really given ". The assumption, in the former case, is that sense-data can be experienced by us without our noticing them, and that they can have sensible properties that we do not immediately detect ; in the other case, it is that, since the character of what we observe is affected by our conscious or unconscious memories of our past experience, it is necessary to discount these associations in order to discover what sense-data are really being sensed. If we accept the first of these assumptions, we have to allow that sense-data can have properties that they do not appear to have. If we accept the second, we have to allow that they can appear to have properties that they do not really have. In both cases, therefore, the tendency is again to assimilate sense-data to material things. But, as we have seen, the utility of the sense-datum language depends upon our being able to make the distinction between sense-data and material things as sharp as possible. We must try, therefore, to avoid these conclusions if we legitimately can.

Let us consider first what reason there can be for holding that not all of what we seem to experience is really given. The cases to which this view is applied are primarily those in which our actual observations are at variance with some physiological theory. One might, for example, be inclined to suppose that the apparent sizes of objects varied with their distance from the observer, or that the colours that they appeared to display varied in accordance with their illumination, or that a change in the position of an object, in relation to the observer, would involve a change in its apparent shape. But these theories are not completely borne out by the empirical facts. We find that a man looks very much the same size at a distance of ten yards as at a distance of five ; and that though, to quote Professor Köhler, " a simple consideration of geometrical optics will tell you that during the man's approach his [apparent] height must have doubled and his breadth too, so that his total size must have become four times the amount it was at ten yards ".[1] We find that a white paper that is seen in the shadow of a screen does not appear the same colour as a black paper that is seen in a full light, even though the amount of light that the two papers reflect is the same. The images that they throw upon the retina of the observer may be equally intense ; but the

---

[1] W. Köhler, *Gestalt Psychology*, p. 36.

white paper still appears to him to be white, and the black paper, black.[1] And this constancy of appearances extends also to shapes. Though philosophers seem inclined to assume that a round object, when it is seen obliquely, always looks elliptical, the empirical fact is that it usually does not. If I look sideways at a coin, the image that it projects upon my retina is indeed elliptical, but in spite of that, the coin still seems to me to be round. And by this I do not mean that, in spite of seeing it as elliptical, I judge the coin to be really round, but that it is a round and not an elliptical shape that I seem actually to see.

Now it is sometimes suggested that the explanation of such phenomena as these is that we doctor our impressions in the light of our past experience. When I look at the coin obliquely, the sense-datum that I am sensing is, it is said, in itself elliptical ; at the same time I know that if I were looking at the coin vertically, my sense-datum would be circular, and I take this as evidence that the coin really is circular in shape ; accordingly, I subconsciously correct my elliptical sense-datum so as to bring it into accord with the " real " shape of the coin. And the other examples are dealt with in the same way. In each case it is assumed that we subconsciously make allowances for the abnormal conditions, and thereby transform the character of the sense-data that we actually sense. In support of this theory it is argued that we can discover what sense-data are really given in these cases by so arranging the conditions that

[1] Cf. Köhler, *op. cit.* p. 58.

we are robbed of our motives for correcting them. Thus, if I know that the white paper is in shadow, and that the black paper is fully exposed to the light, it is held that I allow this knowledge to affect the character of my sense-data, and that it is for this reason that the difference in the colour of the two pieces of paper appears to be reproduced in my sense-data, even though the papers are actually reflecting an equal amount of light. But if I isolate the pieces of paper from their visual context by, for example, interposing a perforated piece of grey cardboard, then, if the papers reflect the same amount of light, the colours of the sense-data by which they are presented will appear approximately the same. And from this it is inferred that even when the pieces of paper are not thus isolated, the sense-data that are actually given are really similar in colour ; and that the difference we appear to see between them is a psychological accretion.

Against this, I may begin by remarking that even as a psychological hypothesis it is open to serious objection. Those who advance it assume that by isolating objects from their actual context, and presenting them in a homogeneous medium, one is able to discover how they would appear to someone whose sensations had not been influenced by past experience. But if, as the *gestalt* psychologists maintain, " the properties of any part of a sense-field depend normally upon the conditions given in the whole field, or, at least, in a larger area of it ",[1] this assump-

---

[1] W. Köhler, *Gestalt Psychology*, p. 72.

tion is unjustified. And experiments such as the one
that I have just described favour the *gestalt* hypothesis
just as much as the other. The fact that the white
paper in one case appears to be similar in colour to
the black, and in the other case does not, though in
each case the two reflect the same amount of light,
proves that our sensations of brightness are not
always completely determined by the intensity of
the corresponding retinal images. But there is
nothing in the evidence to show that the additional
factor is to be sought in the influence of past experience rather than in the character of the present
environment. Admittedly, there is good empirical
evidence for holding that our past experience does
very often affect the character of our sense-data. To
take a simple example, one finds when one learns a
foreign language that its signs do sensibly alter their
look and sound, as one grows more familiar with
their meaning. But it cannot be inferred from this
that whenever our sense-data appear to have different
properties from those that we should expect them
to have, if their character depended exclusively on
" local stimulation ", the difference can be wholly
accounted for by supposing that we correct them in
the light of our past experience. Not only can we
not simply rule out the *gestalt* hypothesis ; we are
not entitled to assume even that the influence of the
subjective attitude of the observer, in determining
the character of his sense-data, must be confined to
this particular process of correction. The physiological theory has the advantage of simplicity ; but

I am not myself convinced that it is adequate to the facts.

In the present context, however, the important point is that even if this theory were adequate to the facts, it still would not make it necessary, or even justifiable, for us to draw a distinction between the properties that sense-data appear to have and those that they really have. Here again the matter at issue is not factual but linguistic. It relates, not to the empirical characteristics of the phenomena in question, but only to the choice of a method for describing them. In this case it is suggested that we should take as our criterion of " reality ", with regard to the properties of sense-data, not what we actually observe, but what it is supposed that we should be observing if it were not for the influence of our past experience. But though this criterion may be work-able, it is surely very inconvenient. If we intend to analyse the " reality " of material things in terms of hypothetical propositions about sense-data, it can only lead to confusion if we bring in another class of hypothetical propositions for the purpose of defining the " reality " of the properties of sense-data themselves. Furthermore, as I have already pointed out, the advantage of having the sense-datum terminology is very much diminished if one allows the distinction between appearance and reality to apply to sense-data, as well as to material things ; for one of its main recommendations is that it is supposed to enable us to escape the puzzlements to which this distinction gives rise. And if, as seems

probable, there is in fact no simple method of dis-
counting the influence of past experience upon our
sensations, the choice of this criterion would involve
the further difficulty that we should very seldom be
able to say what the properties of our sense-data
really were. These objections would indeed have
to be disregarded if there were no other way of
describing the relevant facts. But this is not the
case. If one makes it a rule that all sense-data really
have the properties that they appear to have, no
matter what may be the causes of their appearing as
they do, one is not in any way debarred from expressing the fact that the character of one's sense-
data may be affected by one's past experience. One
may express it by saying that, given a set of conditions
which includes the effects of past experience, the
sense-data that a person senses may be different from
those that he would be sensing if the relevant
conditions did not include this factor. But I do not
infer from this that the properties which would be
affected by the alteration in the conditions do not
really characterize the sense-data which they appear
to characterize. For this would be to admit a distinction to which I attach no meaning when it is
applied to sense-data. According to the convention
which I am adopting (and I have made it clear that
there is nothing here at issue except a choice of conventions) in the domain of sense-data whatever
appears is real.

To show how this convention operates, I shall
now make use of an example which was given to me,

in the form of a problem, by Mr. Gilbert Ryle. It is a popular belief that when a man is struck with sufficient force he may have an experience which is described as the experience of seeing stars. Suppose that this happens to someone we know and that we ask him how many stars he saw. He may have to reply that while he was conscious of seeing stars he was not aware of them as constituting a definite number. We may then be tempted to assert that if he saw stars at all he must have seen a definite number; but that perhaps he was too dizzy to count them. But this would be a mistake. We should be assuming unjustifiably that what could be said about material things could also be said about sense-data. It is true that if the stars in question were physical objects, there would be a definite number of them, whether the observer was aware of it or not. But if we use the expression " seeing stars " to refer only to the sensing of certain sense-data, then, if the sense-data do not appear to be enumerable, they really are not enumerable. No doubt, if our observer had been less dizzy he might have seen, not just a mass of stars, but a definite number. But this does not imply that his experience was not what he took it to be; that he was really seeing a definite number of stars, though all that he was conscious of was an indefinite mass. It implies only that in different conditions he might have had a qualitatively different experience. And the situation would be the same if we assumed that he was looking at the stars, in the ordinary sense. So long as we were referring to them as material things, it would be meaningful for us to say that he was really seeing a definite number of stars although he was not conscious of it ; but no such statement could significantly be made about the sense-data by means of which the stars were presented to him. For a group of sense-data can be said to be enumerable only if it is in fact enumerated. And to say that it might have been enumerated, though actually it was not, is not to say that it had any undetected property, but only that some other group, which would have been enumerable, might have occurred in its place.

By refusing to draw a distinction between that which is really given to an observer and that which he is aware of, I exclude also the possibility of their being sense-data whose existence is not noticed at the time that they are sensed. To illustrate the kind of fact that makes philosophers inclined to admit this possibility I may take an example from the work of Professor Broad.[1] He points out that we sometimes have the experience of " looking for something, failing to find it, and yet discovering afterwards that it had been staring one in the face in the very drawer in which we have been looking ", and he goes on to consider whether in such a case there are good grounds for saying that we were unconsciously perceiving the object in question. He states the arguments in favour of this view as follows : " If I had recognized at the time that I was perceiving the

---

[1] *The Mind and its Place in Nature*, pp. 410-15.

E 2

object, I should certainly have found it. As I did not find it, it seems reasonable to suppose either that I was not perceiving it at all or that, if I was, this perception was not noticed by me. Now, if it existed, it is hardly likely to have escaped my notice by mere inadvertence; for this was the very experience which I was wanting and expecting at the time. . . . [But] the object was in such a position that light from it must have affected the central part of my retina; and, therefore, it is very unlikely that it did not produce a perceptual experience at all. Lastly, it might be that in some cases we could add to this presumption something further of the following kind: Last night I dreamed of the object in a certain place in the drawer; and when I went this morning and looked again, there it was. Or again: I was hypnotized afterwards and told the hypnotist where the object was and he found it there. We should then have a pretty strong case, superficially at any rate, for the view that I had a literally unconscious perception of this object when I was looking for it in the drawer."

Professor Broad himself denies that these arguments establish the desired conclusion. He admits that they " make it highly probable that, if a perception existed at the time, it was literally unconscious relatively to the mind which was then controlling the body at any rate ". But he does not see that there is " any reason to believe that a perception of this object existed at all ". He says, however, that it seems to him likely that in cases of this kind " there really was a sensum in the visual field, which was, in fact, an appearance of the object that we were seeking ; but that for some reason the traces which would usually be excited under such conditions were not excited, or, if they were, failed to produce their normal effect. This sensum was therefore not selected and discriminated from the rest of the field, and was not recognized as an appearance of the object for which we were looking." But if this is his view it is doubtful whether he really disagrees with those who maintain that the object in question was unconsciously perceived. He denies that it was unconsciously perceived because he uses the word " perception " in such a way that an object cannot be said to be perceived, even unconsciously, unless some sensum is actually recognized as an appearance of it. But I doubt if those who believe in the existence of unconscious perceptions do understand the word " perception " in this way. I think that in their view, to admit that there really was a sensum in the visual field which was in fact an appearance of the object, although not recognized as such, would be tantamount to admitting that the object was unconsciously perceived.

For my part, I do not make this admission. Assuming that the word " sensum " is understood to mean what I mean by " sense-datum ", I simply deny that there really was such a sensum in the visual field. My ground for this denial is admittedly conventional. I do not attach any meaning to the statement that among the sense-data that made up an experienced sense-field there existed one that was not sensed. But it must be understood that, in adhering to this convention, I am not denying any empirical fact. The empirical facts are that the object was in such a physical relation to the observer's body that in normal circumstances we should expect him to have perceived it, and that subsequently he seems to remember that he did perceive it. If, in spite of this, he was not, at the time when he was supposed to be perceiving it, aware of any sense-datum that belonged to the object, it may be concluded, first, that one's awareness of visual sense-data is not wholly determined by such physical factors as the affection of the retina, and secondly, that it is possible to have the experience of seeming to remember what one has, in fact, not previously sensed. To maintain that there must really have been a sense-datum of the object in the observer's visual field, although he was not conscious of it, is not to account for the facts in any way, but is merely to adopt an alternative criterion of what is to constitute the existence of a sense-datum. It is to suggest that, instead of making our awareness of a sense-datum the only criterion of its existence, we should say also that a sense-datum exists, or at least that it has existed, when certain physical conditions are fulfilled, or when we have the experience of seeming to remember it. But I do not see any reason to accept either of these proposals. The use of a physiological criterion for determining the existence of sense-data is objectionable because it tempts us to fall into the confusions that result from treating sense-data as a species of material things. And while the adoption of the memory criterion may not in itself be a source of serious confusion, it introduces a complication into the sense-datum language without, so far as I can see, securing any compensatory advantage.

The question which remains still to be considered is whether sense-data can ever really have properties that they do not appear to have. It has been asserted, for example by Professor Broad, that while " sensa cannot appear to have properties they do not really have, there is no reason why they should not have more properties than we can or do notice in them ". " We must distinguish ", he says, " between failing to notice what is present in an object and ' noticing ' what is not present in an object. The former presents no special difficulty. There may well be an object which is too minute and obscure for us to recognize distinctly. Again, it is obvious that we may sense an object without necessarily being aware of all its relations even to another object that we sense at the same time. Consequently, there is no difficulty whatever in supposing that sensa may be much more differentiated than we think them to be, and that two sensa may really differ in quality when we think that they are exactly alike." [1] The second of these points has been made more strongly by Bertrand Russell. " It is important to realize ", he says, " that two sense-data may be, and *must*

[1] *Scientific Thought*, p. 244.

sometimes be, really different when we cannot perceive any difference between them." [1]

The ground upon which it is maintained that " a sense-datum with which I am acquainted may perfectly well have parts with which I am not acquainted " [2] is, presumably, that if I scrutinize the sense-datum more carefully, or examine it with the help of instruments, I may detect features in it that I have not been able to detect before. But why, we must ask, should it be supposed that the sense-datum which I sense in these new conditions is the same as that which I was sensing before they were introduced ? The answer, in this case also, depends upon the choice of a convention. If one defines " the given " physiologically, then it is reasonable to postulate that a change in the attitude of the observer shall not be regarded as involving any change in the nature of the sense-datum that he observes. But if one rejects the purely physiological criterion, as I have found reason to do, it is preferable to say, not that a more exact scrutiny reveals parts of a sense-datum that were not apparent before, but rather that it causes one sense-datum to be replaced by another which resembles the first but is more highly differentiated. Thus, while it can be true of a material thing that it is too minute and obscure for us to recognize properly, I deny that this can be true of a sense-datum. By looking through a microscope I may dis-

[1] *Our Knowledge of the External World*, p. 141.
[2] C. D. Broad, " Is there 'Knowledge by Acquaintance'?" *Aristotelian Society Supplementary Proceedings*, 1919, p. 218.

cover that some material thing has properties that I
have not previously detected in it ; but I should not
express any fact of this kind by saying that I found
some of my sense-data to have properties that they
did not previously appear to have. For while the
material thing remains the same whether or not I
make use of a microscope to observe it, the sense-
data do not. And the reason for this is that I choose
to say, not that the use of the microscope enables
people to detect new features of sense-data which
they were already apprehending, but that it leads
them to apprehend new sense-data. I adopt the
convention that reinforces the distinction between
sense-data and material things, in preference to one
that would encourage us to confuse them.

In support of his view that two sense-data must
sometimes be really different when we cannot perceive any difference between them, Russell argues
as follows : " In all cases of sense-data capable of
gradual change, we may find one sense-datum
indistinguishable from another, and that other
indistinguishable from a third, while yet the first and
third are quite easily distinguishable. Suppose, for
example, a person with his eyes shut is holding a
weight in his hand, and someone noiselessly adds a
small extra weight. If the extra weight is small
enough, no difference will be perceived in the sensation. After a time, another small extra weight may
be added, and still no change will be perceived ; but
if both extra weights had been added at once, it may
be that the change would be quite easily perceptible.

Or, again, take shades of colour. It would be easy to find three stuffs of such closely similar shades that no difference could be perceived between the first and second, nor yet between the second and third, while yet the first and third would be distinguishable. In such a case, the second shade cannot be the same as the first, or it would be distinguishable from the third ; nor the same as the third, or it would be distinguishable from the first. It must therefore, though indistinguishable from both, be really intermediate between them." [1]

There is no reason to dispute the empirical facts that are set forth in this argument ; but the conclusion Russell draws does not follow from them. The question is whether the relation of exact resemblance, in respect of colour, or weight, or any other sensible property, is to be regarded as applying to sense-data in the same way as it applies to material things. When it is applied to material things this relation is understood to be both symmetrical and transitive. That is to say, if a material thing A is characterized, for example, by exactly the same shade of colour as another material thing B, then it follows not only that B is characterized by exactly the same shade of colour as A, but also that if B is of exactly the same shade as a third thing C, A too is of exactly the same shade as C. But it must not be assumed that this principle will hold good also for sense-data. For the logical counterpart of a relation between sense-data is not a relation that really characterizes

<hr>

[1] *Our Knowledge of the External World*, pp. 141-2.

material things, but only one that appears to characterize them. To say that a sense-datum a, which belongs to a material thing A, has the relation R to a sense-datum b, which belongs to a material thing B, is not to say that A really has R to B, but only that it appears to have R to B. Accordingly, the model that we must take for the relation of exact resemblance between sense-data is not the relation of exact resemblance between material things, but the relation between material things of appearing to be exactly resemblant ; and this relation, though it too is symmetrical, is not transitive. For it is admitted that a material thing A can appear exactly to resemble a second thing B, and that B can appear exactly to resemble a third thing C, in respect of some sensible property, without its being the case that A and C appear in this respect exactly to resemble one another. We must therefore conclude that the relation of exact resemblance is not a transitive relation when it is applied to sense-data. Or, if it be objected that a non-transitive relation of exact resemblance is a contradiction in terms, we must say that the relation of exact resemblance does not apply at all to sense-data, and then we must find some other name for the relation that obtains between two sense-data when the corresponding material things appear exactly to resemble one another. In either case, we destroy the ground for holding that sense-data must sometimes differ in ways that are not apparent. For the assumption that there really obtains between sense-data, as between material things, a relation of exact resemblance which is both symmetrical and transitive is indispensable to Russell's argument.

We see then that the facts that have led certain philosophers to hold that the distinction between appearance and reality must apply to sense-data, as well as to material things, do not necessitate this conclusion. It is indeed open to these philosophers to formulate the rules of the sense-datum language in such a way as to admit this distinction, if they choose ; but I have shown that it is much more convenient to exclude it. From the conventions which I am adopting it follows that one's awareness of a sense-datum cannot be delusive in the way that one's perception of a material thing can. If one knows what properties a sense-datum appears to have, one knows what properties it really has. This does not prevent us, however, from expressing false propositions even about the sense-data that we are actually sensing. For it is always possible, whether from an intention to deceive or else because of a verbal error, to misdescribe the properties that they appear to have.

A further point in favour of this way of conceiving " the given " is that it imposes no *a priori* restrictions upon the possible scope of perceptual knowledge. It might be thought that in saying that perceiving a material thing always involved being directly aware of a sense-datum, I was making it a necessary condition for a material thing to be veridically perceived that it should exercise some physical stimulus upon a sense-organ, and was thus excluding the possibility of clairvoyance as a method of perception.

But this is not the case.   It may indeed be questioned whether much of what is now referred to as " extra-sensory perception "[1] ought properly to be called " perception " at all.   I at least should prefer not to extend the use of the term " perception " to cover those cases in which the object that is supposed to be perceived is not located by the percipient anywhere in physical space.   But if there are experiences that are held to be extra-sensory, not because they seem to differ intrinsically from sensory perceptions, but because of a difference in the conditions of their occurrence, then I think they may reasonably be counted as perceptions.   And if one allows them to be perceptions, then one may describe them in terms of sense-data.   For I am using the word " sense-datum " in such a way that in every case in which it can legitimately be said that a material thing is being perceived it can also be said that a sense-datum is being sensed.   It makes no difference what the causes of the perception may be.   In determining the existence and character of sense-data we must consider only what it is that is actually observed ; the question how it comes to be observed is irrelevant. In this way we ensure that " the theory of sense-data " does not involve more than the elaboration of a special terminology for describing our perceptual experience.   It must not be regarded as presupposing the validity of any particular theory either about the causes or about the character of what we perceive or sense.

[1] Cf. J. B. Rhine, *Extra-Sensory Perception*.

III

THE EGOCENTRIC PREDICAMENT

12. THE PRIVACY OF PERSONAL EXPERIENCE

A PROPOSITION the truth of which is often taken for granted in discussions on the theory of knowledge is that one can directly experience only what is private to oneself. It is, however, recognized that every sane man assumes, in practice, that there do exist other human beings besides himself, and furthermore that he and they inhabit a common world. He may agree that they are not able to have numerically the same feelings as he has, or to sense the same sense-data, but he believes that they can, at any rate, perceive the same material things. Now few, if any, philosophers are prepared to hold that these assumptions are unwarranted, but they have found it difficult to justify them in view of the supposed privacy of immediate experience. And for empiricists this problem is thought to be especially acute. How, for example, can we hold it to be possible to express perceptual judgements in terms of sense-data if we are obliged to deny that any sense-datum can be experienced by more than one person ? Have I indeed any ground for believing that there can be sense-data apart from those that I sense myself ? And how can a number of sets of private sense-data conceivably make up a common, public world ?

To illustrate the point of view of those who believe that a theory of knowledge must necessarily be based upon the individual's private experience, I may quote from a recent work by Professor W. T. Stace.[1] " I cannot experience ", says Professor Stace, " anything except *my own* experience. I can see my red but I can never see yours. I can feel a pain in my leg. But I can never feel the pain in your leg. I can feel my emotion but not yours. Even if your anger infects me, so that I feel it in sympathy with you, it is yet, in so far as I feel it, *my* anger, not yours. I can never be you, nor you me. I cannot see through your eyes, nor you through mine. Even if you can telepathically transfer a mental state, say an image, from your mind to mine, yet when I become aware of it, it is then *my* image and not yours. Even if, as some think, I can directly perceive your mind, without having to infer it from your body, still this perception of your mind will then be to me *my* perception, *my* experience."

" All knowledge ", he continues, " all philosophy must be based upon experience. And from whose experience can I begin except from my own ? Whatever belief I hold on whatever subject must be either a datum of *my* consciousness or else an inference or mental construction which *I* base upon *my* data. If

[1] *Theory of Knowledge and Existence*, p. 67.

I accept a scientific belief on your authority, this belief must be an inference which I make from the sounds (words) I hear you utter, and from *my* belief in your repute as a scientific authority. Whatever I believe rests in the end upon the data of my own consciousness. Therefore all knowledge must have had its beginning in my own self-enclosed personal experience. This original solipsism is utterly unescapable except by prejudice or refusing to see it."

With one exception, to which I shall presently refer, my criticism of these propositions is not that they are false, or even dubious, but rather that they are trivial. For what is it, after all, that prevents one person from having the experiences of another ? Why is it impossible for me to have someone else's pains, or to feel his emotions, or, in general, to " experience anything except my own experience " ? This is not a case of a physical incapacity, like my inability to see through a brick wall, or of a psychological incapacity, such as my inability to remember all the events of my childhood. The barriers that prevent us from enjoying one another's experiences are not natural but logical. It is conceivable that there should be people who were capable of seeing through brick walls, or that there should be people who were capable of remembering every detail of their pasts, but it is not conceivable that there should be people who were capable of having one another's pains, or feeling one another's emotions. And the reason why this is inconceivable is simply that we attach no meaning to such expressions as " I am experiencing your headache ", " She is feeling his remorse ", " Your state of anger is numerically the same as mine ". It is necessary to insert the word " numerically " in the last example, in order to allow for the fact that there is a sense in which it can be said that different people do have common experiences. We frequently use such sentences as " He shares my indignation at your conduct ", " My emotions on hearing his story were the same as yours ", " I am drawn to him because we have so many tastes in common " ; and when philosophers assert that each man's experiences are private to himself they do not, presumably, wish to deny that sentences of this kind are intelligible, or even that they often express true propositions. They would say, however, that all that was meant in such cases was that different people's experiences were qualitatively alike, or that they proceeded from similar causes. What they would deny is that the experiences of two different people could ever be numerically the same, as, for example, the pen with which I am writing is numerically the same as that with which I was writing yesterday, or as Charles Edward Stuart was numerically the same person as the Young Pretender. They would maintain that whatever relation an experience of mine might have to that of another person, it would still be exclusively my experience, and that, being mine, it could not also be someone else's. For it is impossible that the same experience should be part of the history of two separate selves. But the reason why this is impossible is simply that there is no usage of such expressions as " being numerically the same " that is applicable to the experiences of two different people. To occur in the history of a different person is, in the sense of " being different " with which we are here concerned, to be a different experience. And from this we may derive analytically the proposition that each person's experience is private to himself.

Having thus traced the privacy of experience to the acceptance of a verbal convention, I may now be faced with the question whether this convention is arbitrary. Surely, it may be said, there is more to this matter than our merely choosing not to speak of numerical identity in connexion with the experiences of different people. The answer is that every verbal convention is arbitrary in the trivial sense that, however we may use words, it is always conceivable that we should have used them otherwise ; but at the same time we do use words to describe matters of fact, and while it is never true of any set of facts that there is one and only one possible way of describing them, it may depend to some extent upon the nature of the facts that we find it convenient to describe them in one way rather than another. In the present case, we do not find it convenient to use expressions that would imply that different people could have numerically identical experiences ; but it is not difficult to imagine circumstances in which we should be inclined to give such expressions a meaning. Consider, for example, Professor Stace's

proposition that " I can never feel the pain in your
leg ". If the pain in your leg is understood to be
a pain that you are feeling, this proposition is
analytically true ; for it is a matter of convention
that any pain that I feel is numerically different from
any pain that is felt by you. It is not, however,
logically necessary that all the pains that a person
feels should be located in his own body. For
suppose that two people, A and B, display signs of
being in pain, and then when they are asked where
the pain is they both point to B's leg ; and suppose,
what may be physically but is not logically impossible,
that when pressure is applied to B's leg A's pain as
well as B's appears to be intensified, and that after
B's leg has been medically treated, A's pain as well
as B's appears to be assuaged. In such a case we
should say that while B was feeling a pain in his own
body, A was feeling a pain not in his own body but
in B's. We should judge that both of them were
feeling pain because we should be able to observe
manifestations of pain in both bodies ; in particular,
the responses to our questions would issue from A's
body as well as B's ; and in these circumstances we
should not hesitate to say that while A's pain
appeared to be located in B's body, it was numerically
different from B's. But it might conceivably be the
case that no manifestations of pain came from A's
body, but that there were other, psychological,
grounds for believing that the pain was nevertheless
felt by A. We might, for instance, observe that the
expressions that B made use of in describing the

pain were characteristic of A, and that, subsequently, A too was able to remember it. If this were to happen, we should still, according to our present conventions, be obliged to say that if A did feel the pain in B's body, the pain which he felt was not numerically the same as that which was felt by B. But I believe that if occurrences of this kind were common we should eventually alter our way of speaking so as to allow, in a case such as that which I am now considering, of there being only a single feeling of pain which was experienced by both A and B. Instead of making it a necessary proposition that the series of experiences that constituted the histories of two different people contained no common members, we should admit the possibility that they could occasionally intersect.

This possibility is made easier to envisage because of the fact that we ordinarily employ two different sets of criteria for determining the ownership of experiences. There are, on the one hand, what may be called the psychological criteria of continuity of disposition and memory. We say that a series of experiences constitutes the history of a single person if similar mental states recur throughout the series in similar conditions, and if, as the series is prolonged, its later sections always contain some experiences that are memories of the earlier. It is the use of these criteria that makes it possible to attach significance to the hypotheses that people survive the dissolution of their bodies, or that they animate different bodies at different times, provided that this survival is

understood to imply no more than the prolongation
of a series of experiences that fulfils the conditions
I have indicated ; for though it may be very improb-
able that there actually is any series of this kind
whose members are not all associated with one particular body, it is not logically impossible that there
should be. Association with a particular body
becomes logically necessary to a person's continued
existence only when we bring in the second set of
criteria by which we determine personal identity, or,
what comes to the same thing, the ownership of
experiences. For we then make the persistence of a
self depend, not upon consistency of character, or
powers of memory, or any other psychological factor,
but simply upon bodily continuity. According to
this way of speaking, an experience is mine if the
total field of consciousness in which it occurs includes
organic sense-data belonging to " my body ", these
organic sense-data being correlated with visual and
tactual sense-data, which are distinguished by the
fact that they always occupy a region of minimum
depth in their respective sense-fields. I need not now
consider the principles according to which these
sense-data may be conceived as constituting a single,
persistent material thing, namely, my body ; for they
are the same as those that govern the analysis of any
other material thing in terms of sense-data, and this
is a question with which I shall be dealing later on.[1]
What concerns me now is the relationship between
the two different methods of determining when an

[1] Part V.

experience is to be accounted the experience of a given person. It happens to be the case that they normally yield the same result. An experience that is proved to be mine by the test of memory and disposition is proved also to be mine by the test of bodily continuity. But while this parallelism may be physically necessary, in virtue of a causal dependence of the psychological upon the somatic factors, it is logically contingent. There would be no contradiction in supposing that there were series of experiences that would be attributable to different people, according as one made use of the psychological or the physical criteria of personal identity. And in this way one is provided with the means of imagining circumstances in which one would be inclined to break down the barriers that conventionally separate one person's experience from another's, as was shown in the simple illustration that I gave.

But however easy it may be to devise a situation in which we should be disposed to alter our manner of speaking about the ownership of experiences, the fact is that, as we use words at present, it must be held to be logically impossible that the series of experiences that constitute the histories of different people should ever intersect. Consequently, when a philosopher like Professor Stace asserts that he can never be another person, and that he can never experience anything except his own experience, he may be understood to be expressing propositions which are analytically true. But it is a different matter when he goes on to assert that " all knowledge must have had its beginning in my own self-enclosed personal experience ". The description of being the first person ever to acquire knowledge may perhaps apply to one of our remote ancestors ; it certainly does not apply to Professor Stace. Moreover, if it were the case that all knowledge had to have its beginning in Professor Stace's self-enclosed personal experience, it would follow that no knowledge could originate in the personal experience of anybody else ; but the theory seems to be that each of us is obliged to hold that " all knowledge must have had its beginning in my own self-enclosed personal experience ", and this is self-contradictory. It may be objected that I am here being unfair to Stace by understanding him too literally, and that all that he really means to assert is the trivial proposition that all *my* knowledge must have had its beginning in my own personal experience, whoever I may be ; but I do not think that this is so. I think that he is deliberately equating " knowledge " with " my knowledge " because he does not see how, if each person is unable to experience anything except his own experience, he can ever have any reason to believe in the existence of any knowledge besides his own. And if this is his difficulty it is one that he shares with many other philosophers. They make statements that seem to imply that there can be no knowledge besides their own, not because they really disbelieve in the existence of other human beings who are also capable of acquiring knowledge, but because they do not see how to make the transition from the individual's " self-enclosed personal experience " to the common, social world.

13. PUBLIC AND PRIVATE LANGUAGES

An alternative way of formulating this problem, which has recently come into favour, is to treat it as question of the inter-relationship of languages. There is, we are told, on the one hand the " physical language " which is said to be " characterized by the fact that statements of the simplest form attach to a specific set of co-ordinates a definite value or range of values of a coefficient of physical state ", or, in other words, " express a quantitatively determined property of a definite position at a definite time "[1] ; and on the other hand there is the " protocol language ", which consists of " statements belonging to the basic protocol or direct record "[2] of an individual's experience. It is assumed that the physical language is inter-subjective ; and the question then is to determine how the protocol language is related to it. The answer that is given by those who use these terms is that the protocol language is a sub-language of the physical language. There is, in their view, no problem involved in making the transition from the realm of the individual's direct experience to the realm of public, physical facts ; for they hold that reports of direct experience themselves already refer to such facts. In considering this view, I may

[1] Rudolf Carnap, *The Unity of Science*, pp. 52-3.
[2] *Ibid.* p. 42.

refer once again to the work of Professor Carnap, who has given the fullest and clearest exposition of it. To prove that the protocol language is a part of the inter-subjective physical language, he uses the following argument. He affects to adopt the standpoint of an opponent who maintains that when he asserts a protocol proposition such as " I am thirsty " he is referring not to a physical event but to the content of one of his experiences. In that case, argues Carnap, the same state of affairs cannot also be expressed in the protocol language of any other person. " No statement in S2's protocol language ", he says, " can express the thirst of S1. For all such statements express only what is immediately given to S2 ; and S1's thirst is a datum for S1 only and not for S2. . . . All that S2 can verify when he asserts ' S1 is thirsty ' is that S1's body is in such and such a state, and a statement asserts no more than can be verified. If by ' the thirst of S1 ' we understand not the physical state of his body but his sensations of thirst, *i.e.* something non-material, then S1's thirst is fundamentally beyond the reach of S2's recognition. A statement about S1's thirst would then be fundamentally unverifiable by S2, it would be for him in principle impossible to understand, void of sense." The same thing would, it is held, be true of every other protocol statement, and the general consequence would be that " every protocol language could be applied only solipsistically ".[1]

---

[1] *Ibid.* pp. 79-80.

The next step in the argument is to consider what, on this view, must be the relationship between protocol and physical statements. If scientific statements are to be capable of being verified empirically there must be some " inferential connexion " between the two ; but how is this possible if " the protocol language and the physical language speak of completely different facts " ? Suppose that we adopt the hypothesis that " although protocol language does not refer to physical events the converse is true and physical language refers to the content of experiences ". Then, it is argued, " difficulties arise on considering the relation between the several persons' protocol languages and physical language. S1's protocol language refers to the content of S1's experience, S2's protocol language to the content of S2's experience. What can the inter-subjective physical language refer to ? It must refer to the content of the experiences of both S1 and S2. This is, however, impossible, for the realms of experience of two persons do not overlap." And so it is concluded that " there is no solution free from contradictions in this direction ".[1]

The solution Carnap himself puts forward is that every protocol statement is equivalent to a statement about the subject's body. For instance, the protocol statement " red now ", made by a subject S, is said to be equivalent to " the body S is now seeing red " where " seeing red " " denotes that state of the human body characterized by the

[1] *The Unity of Science*, pp. 81-2.

fact that certain specified (physical) reactions appear
in answer to certain specified (physical) stimuli.
(For example ; Stimulus ; the sounds, ' What do you
see now ? ' reaction ; the sound, ' red '. Stimulus,
the sounds, ' Point out the colour you have just seen
on this card ' ; reaction ; the finger points to some
definite part of the card . . .)." [1] In this way every
protocol statement is given an interpretation that
allows it to be incorporated in the physical language.
The protocol languages of various persons are said
to be mutually exclusive only in the sense that " they
are non-overlapping sub-sections of the physical
language ".[2] Each person's protocol statements are
supposed to refer to the states of his own body, and
so to a special class of physical facts.

It is Carnap's view that the problem of the
egocentric predicament, which he solves in this
fashion, would never have troubled philosophers if
they had expressed it, in " formal " terminology, as
a question about the relationship of languages instead
of speaking, in " material " terms, about the contents
of people's experiences and their relation to the
public world. But in this instance his predilection
for the formal terminology has led him into confusion. His argument rests, as we have seen, upon
the assumption that if the sentences of the protocol
language referred, not to physical events, but to the
contents of experiences, it would follow, in view of
the privacy of personal experience, that each person
would have his own private protocol language which

---

[1] *Ibid.* p. 86.   [2] *Ibid.* p. 88.

F

could have no meaning for anybody else. But this assumption is false. It is due to a mistranslation from the material into the formal mode of speech. A correct formal rendering of the proposition that each person's experiences are private to himself might run as follows : " For any experience E, and personal histories H_1 and H_2, ' E belongs to H_1 ' implies that E does not belong to H_2 ". And this is by no means equivalent, as Carnap seems to suppose, to saying that each person has his own protocol language, when this is taken to mean that " for any protocol sentence s, and persons A and B, ' s occurs in the language used by A ' implies that s does not occur in the language used by B ". Nor does this proposition asserting the privacy of each person's protocol language follow from the proposition that the sentences of the protocol language refer to the contents of experiences. It is indeed possible to have a private protocol language, just as it is possible to have a private physical language. If, for example, I were to express propositions about the contents of my experiences by executing the movements of a dance, and no one else made these movements in order to express such propositions, I might correctly be said to be using a private protocol language ; and similarly, if I were to whistle snatches of popular tunes in order to express propositions about physical events, and no one else expressed such propositions in this way, I might correctly be said to be using a private physical language. But it is no more necessary for me to express protocol propositions in a private language than it is for me to express physical propositions in a private language. When I employ expressions like " this is red " or " I am thirsty " to refer to the contents of my experiences, I am using English sentences in the way that other English people use them. And, as such sentences are ordinarily used, they are not equivalent to the sentences referring to physical events into which it is proposed that we should translate them. There may indeed be a *de facto* connexion between my feeling of thirst and such physical facts as that my throat is parched or that I utter certain words, or a *de facto* connexion between my sensing a red sense-datum and my being in the physical state that the sentence " my body is seeing red " is intended to describe. But in all such cases, the dependence of the facts referred to by the protocol propositions upon the facts referred to by the physical propositions is logically a contingent and not a necessary relation. Even if one assumed, what is by no means fully established, that to every fact described by a protocol proposition there was a physical correlate, there would still be no logical contradiction involved in asserting the protocol proposition and denying the physical proposition which was empirically conjoined with it. In other words, it is logically conceivable that the protocol proposition should be true when the corresponding physical proposition was false ; and if this is so, the sentences that express them are not equivalent.

We have seen that the ground on which it is

assumed that sentences which seem to refer to the contents of experiences must really refer to physical events is that only thus could they serve as a means of communication between one person and another. But if there is a philosophical problem concerning the possibility of such communication it applies just as much to propositions about physical events as it does to propositions about people's states of mind, or about the sense-data which they directly experience. For it is only in terms of what we individually experience that these physical propositions can be understood by us at all. Suppose, for example, that I wish to ascertain the temperature of the room in which I am sitting, and that, taking up a Fahrenheit thermometer, I observe that the top of the column of mercury coincides with the figure 70. In that case I may put forward the physical proposition that the temperature of the room is 70 degrees Fahrenheit. And if someone else then takes the thermometer and also observes that the top of the mercury column coincides with the figure 70, it may be said that this physical proposition has been inter-subjectively verified. But this inter-subjective verification amounts to no more than what may be described by saying that each of us apprehends a spatial coincidence of two sense-data in his own sense-field. Consequently, since the truth of every physical proposition depends upon the truth of protocol propositions, if the privacy of experience made it impossible for two people to communicate by means of protocol propositions, it would equally be impossible for them to communicate by means of physical propositions. But the fact is that if what is meant by " inter-subjective understanding " is understanding in the same way by a number of different people, both these types of propositions are capable of being inter-subjectively understood.

14. CONCERNING THE PRIVACY OF SENSE-DATA AND THE PUBLICITY OF THE MATERIAL WORLD

There is, however, a sense in which the distinguishing of physical propositions, as inter-subjective, from protocol propositions, as private to each observer, may be held to be justified. It is justifiable if it is understood to imply no more than that we do attach meaning to the statement that different people observe numerically the same physical event or perceive numerically the same material thing, whereas we do not attach any meaning to the statement that different people are characterized by numerically the same mental states. And if, in accordance with this method of classification, we include sentences referring to sense-data in the protocol language, this implies that we have resolved not to attach any meaning to the statement that different observers sense the same sense-datum. Here again, it must be noted that in asserting the privacy of sense-data one is not acknowledging an empirical fact but laying down a verbal convention. It is indeed quite commonly said not only that different people perceive the same material thing, but also that they hear the same sound, or that they see the same colour, in cases where the sound or colour is understood to be a sensible and not a physical characteristic; and if we chose to bring the rules of the sense-datum language into conformity with this usage, we should allow a meaning to the statement that different observers might sense numerically the same sense-datum. But what philosophers who employ the terminology of sense-data usually prefer to say in such cases is that the sounds that are heard, or the colours that are seen, by different observers are not literally the same. They are numerically distinct sense-data, which are said to be the same only in virtue of their having some such relationship to one another as that of qualitative similarity. Whether or not one continues to regard such relations as constituting " sameness " is immaterial. For when philosophers assert that each person's sense-data are necessarily private to himself, it is not according to these relational criteria that they are denying that the sense-data of different observers can be the same, but only in a different sense of " sameness ", which they have themselves introduced and have chosen to regard as fundamental. Their procedure has, in fact, been to extend to sense-data the usage of " literal " or " numerical identity ", by which, as I have shown, it is made impossible for the histories of two different people to overlap. The advantages of this are that it further ensures us against the danger of treating sense-data as if they were a special kind of material things, and that it is more in accordance with the conception of a sense-datum as something immediately " given ". We may therefore accept it as a convention that the sense-data that are sensed by any individual observer are numerically distinct from those that can be sensed by anybody else.

To this it may perhaps be objected that to make each person's sense-data private to himself is altogether to exclude the possibility of giving any kind of phenomenalistic analysis of the material world. For we conceive of material things as being simultaneously accessible to many different observers; and how, it may be asked, can such objects possibly be constituted out of a number of mutually exclusive sets of private sense-data ? A superior being who had access to everybody's sense-data might be able to achieve this construction ; but surely none of us can achieve it, for the only sense-data that any one of us is able to draw on are his own. According to this view, we are in the situation of people who seek to build a house with materials of many different sorts ; each person has access in the territory that he occupies to one of the requisite materials, but no one can obtain the materials that are owned by anybody else, and, since no one can leave his own territory, there is no method of putting the materials into a common fund. Consequently, only the Master Builder who is able to roam all over the various territories and take from them whatever he wants is in a position to build the house ; and then only in some mysterious territory of his own. If this were a fair illustration of it, the problem of " constructing " material things out of sense-data would certainly be insoluble. But it is not a fair illustration and the objection which it supports is ill-founded. There is no question here, as in the case of a physical process of construction, of our creating any objects that did not exist before. The facts we express by referring to sense-data are, for the most part, the same as those that we ordinarily express by referring to material things. And all that is meant by speaking of " construction " or " analysis " in this case is that one terminology is to be exhibited as a function of the other. To this extent, the philosophers who maintain that this is a matter of the inter-relationship of languages are in the right. But they fall into confusion, as I have shown, when they make the transition from the material to the formal mode of speech merely by substituting the expressions " private protocol language " and " public physical language " for " private sense-data " and " public physical objects ", or " events ". For it is no more possible to put together a number of independent private languages so as to form a public language than it is to put together sets of private objects to form a public object, when this is conceived as a task of combining materials that cannot, by any conceivable means, be brought together. But, in fact, the protocol or pheno-menalistic language in terms of which we seek to re-express the statements that we make about material things must not be regarded as the property of any particular person. Our problem is to show what propositions concerning material things amount to in terms of the contents of sensory experience, but not in terms of the experience of any one person rather than any other. It is analogous to setting out the rules of a game, which is a task that can be accomplished equally well whether the game is intended for a number of people to play together or for one person to play by himself. To say that it is impossible to construct material things out of sense-data, because sense-data are private and material things are not, is like saying that it is impossible to give universal rules for playing solitaire or patience, because these are games that one plays by oneself. To obtain a closer analogy, imagine a game of solitary patience in which each person is supposed to have his own special pack of cards, and no one is allowed to play with a pack that has been used by anybody else. The rules of this game would be inter-subjectively valid in the sense that they could be followed by any person who happened to possess the requisite cards ; but the question whether there actually were any such persons would not affect the possibility of framing these rules. In the same way, the possibility of setting forth the principles according to which the material world is " constructed " out of sense-data is not affected by the question whether or not there actually is a set of persons who all experience the requisite sense-data. Admittedly, if I am the one who is to formulate these principles,

I shall have to draw upon my own sensory experience and my own understanding of words; and if, through their failing to experience the necessary sense-data or for some other cause, other people did not understand either the physical or the sensory terms that I was using in the way in which I understood them, my " construction " would be valid only for myself. But this does not mean that I have to put it forward as referring specifically to my experience, any more than the doubt whether any other person possessed a suitable pack of cards would make it necessary for me, in formulating the rules of the game of patience, to speak of it as a game that I myself was able to play. Nor do I, in fact, believe that my " construction " will be valid only for myself. On the contrary, I frequently observe that other people make signs which tally with those that I should use to describe what I am myself experiencing; and that my use of physical or sensory terms evokes from them what I consider to be an appropriate response; and this I regard as evidence that they understand words in the same way as I do. For it is in the satisfaction of criteria of this sort that " understanding words in the same way " conventionally consists.

Before I leave this question, I may note that when someone asserts that everything he says refers exclusively to his own experience, he is not expressing a proposition that is necessarily false. He may, conceivably, be such an egotist that he does, in fact, talk only about himself. But such a man would

be abnormal; and the fact that we can recognize
his abnormality, and that we can draw a distinction
between him and the common run of men who are
not such egotists as this, shows that the philosophers
who maintain that it is impossible for anyone to talk
about anything except his own experience have
fallen into confusion. I have shown what it is that
tempts us to make assertions of this kind; and to
remove this temptation, rather than to establish any
particular thesis, has been the purpose of my
arguments.

Once we are rid of such confusions, it is not
difficult to see how it is possible for material things to
be public, even though sense-data are not. We have
only to ask ourselves what in fact are the criteria by
which we determine when two people are, and when
they are not, perceiving the same material thing.
The commonest procedure is to see whether they
agree in their manner of describing it. Suppose,
for example, that I ask someone what he thinks of
my new picture and he replies that it is an attractive
landscape, or that I have done well to hang it over
the mantelpiece. If these descriptions of " being a
landscape " and " being hung over the mantelpiece "
apply to what I myself am seeing, I judge that he
and I are perceiving the same picture; and my
confidence in this judgement will be strengthened
if he goes on to speak of the form, or colour, or
subject matter of the picture in a way that tallies
with my own observations. It may be, however,
that his remarks do not, as I understand them,

apply to the picture that I am looking at, but that they do seem to me to apply to some other object in the room, and in that case I may judge that we are perceiving different material things. Or it may be that his remarks do not, as I understand them, apply to anything that I am able to observe ; and then I may judge that he is playing a trick on me, or that he is using words in an esoteric way, or that one of us is the victim of an illusion. Which of these alternatives is to be accepted is a question that may be decided by further observation of his behaviour. If I discover, for example, that where other people use the word " red ", he consistently uses the word " green ", I shall not regard the fact that he describes as being green a part of the picture that seems to me to be red as evidence against the proposition that we are perceiving numerically the same picture. The most important factor in such cases is the determination of spatial position ; and this admits of other tests than that of verbal agreement. If I am left in doubt by what another person says as to whether he is referring to the same object as I am, I may ask him to touch the object that he is referring to ; and if I then observe what appears to be a coincidence between the tip of his finger and the appropriate object, I have evidence that although we are sensing different sense-data we are perceiving the same material thing. But do tests of this kind establish more, it may be asked, than that our separate private worlds have a similar structure ? And is not this consistent with their being entirely different in content ? Might it not be the case that if, *per impossibile*, I were in a position to sense someone else's sense-data, I should find that although his use of words appeared to agree with mine, the objects for which he used them were not even qualitatively the same ? The answer is that even if this is true it is not to the purpose. If someone chooses to say that what we regard as a common world is really a set of private worlds which can be known, at best, only to have certain structural properties in common, he is not raising a question that can be decided by any reference to matters of fact. What he is doing is to reject the ordinary usage of such expressions as " you and I are perceiving the same material thing " in favour of some special philosophical usage of his own. But all that I have been concerned to show is that, as such expressions are ordinarily used, our inhabiting a common world is in no way inconsistent with the privacy of our individual experiences. In the sense in which it is normally understood, the proposition that some other person is perceiving a material thing which is numerically the same as that which he is perceiving himself is one whose truth each person can determine by reference to his own sense-data. And it is not necessary, even if it were possible, that he should have access to the sense-data that are sensed by anybody else.

15. THE HYPOTHESIS OF THE EXISTENCE
OF OTHER PEOPLE'S EXPERIENCES

The question that remains to be considered is what evidence anyone has for believing that other people have thoughts or feelings, or sense sense-data that he cannot himself observe. The usual view is that beliefs about the " experiences of other minds " can be justified by an argument from analogy. I know that my own behaviour, and in particular my own use of signs, is correlated with certain experiences ; and this gives me grounds for inferring, when I observe other people behaving in the same ways as I do, that they are having experiences which are similar to my own. But to this it has been objected that although I can legitimately use an analogical argument to establish the existence of something which I cannot in fact observe because of some natural hindrance, I cannot legitimately use any such argument to establish the existence of something which it is logically inconceivable that I should observe. And the contents of other people's experiences are, it is said, in this second category, inasmuch as they are not even in principle accessible to my observation. For have I not acknowledged that it is not even meaningful to say that one person literally shares another's thoughts or memories or emotions, or senses his sense-data, or feels his pleasures and pains ? Accordingly, it is held by those who adopt this standpoint that if one is to be able to attach meaning to statements about other people's experiences they must be interpreted behaviouristically.[1] On this view, I can draw a distinction between my own thoughts and feelings and their physical manifestations, but I cannot maintain this distinction when I am speaking about other people ; for then the physical manifestations are all that I can in principle observe, and therefore all that I can significantly refer to. Indeed it is misleading to use the word " manifestation " at all in this connexion. For it implies that there is something to be manifested, whereas the theory is that for any outside observer the experiences of other people are constituted by their manifestations. There can be empirical grounds for inferring the occurrence of behaviour, on the part of other people, which one is not actually observing, inasmuch as it is logically conceivable that one should observe it ; but there cannot, on this view, be any empirical grounds for inferring the existence of anything " behind " this behaviour of which it might be supposed to be an external manifestation. And the reason that is offered for this is not just that the evidence is lacking, but that no inductive argument can possibly establish a conclusion that is in itself devoid of meaning.

I have heard it suggested that the fact that " one cannot observe the experiences of another person " makes it necessary to admit that there is an irrational element even in the physical sciences.[2] For the

---

[1] This was formerly my own view. Cf. *Language, Truth and Logic*, ch. vii.

[2] Cf. E. Schroedinger, " Quelques remarques au sujet des bases de la connaissance scientifique ", *Scientia*, vol. lvii.

development of these sciences is a social activity. In formulating his theories, each individual scientist assumes the truth of many empirical propositions that he has not himself attempted to verify ; it is sufficient for him to know that the experiments have been made by other observers whose reports he trusts. But if he has no reason to believe that there are any other observers, in the sense in which he knows himself to be an observer, then, it is argued, he has no right to assume the truth of any propositions but those that he has, directly or indirectly, verified himself ; and their number must be comparatively small. It may indeed be answered that the limitation is in any case practical and not logical. For although, in practice, no single person may have the time or the resources to recreate for himself the whole of what he has been accustomed to regard as the generally accepted system of physical knowledge, the feat is not theoretically impossible. But, in fact, the entire argument is invalid. All that a physicist need assume for it to be rational for him to rely upon the findings of another " observer " is that the reports which come from a given source do, as he understands them, record what in suitable conditions he could himself observe ; and this assumption he can justify inductively by testing a certain number of these reports. As far as their fruitfulness is concerned, it need not matter to him how such reports are produced. He can treat them as physical facts, like the marks on photographic plates, or the stratification of rocks. Regarding them simply as a basis for inference, he is not called upon to draw any distinction between the signs that seem to be made deliberately by other human beings and those that he derives from nature or from machines. In each case the question of their reliability for his purpose depends only upon his being able to establish inductive correlations between them and other sense-data. He may in fact make the assumption that some of these signs are produced by people who have experiences which are analogous to his own. But if he wishes only to have reason to believe in the propositions of the physical sciences, this assumption is superfluous.

With regard to what are sometimes called the mental sciences, the position is not so clear. Certainly, no psychologist believes that the laws which he formulates apply only to himself. Nevertheless, I think it can be argued that he does not require the assumption that there are other people who have experiences which are analogous to his own, either for the formulation of his laws, or for their justification. Let us take, for example, Fechner's law that the intensity of a sensation is proportionate to the logarithm of the stimulus. This law is stated impersonally. It does not in any way specify the persons who are supposed to have the sensations in question, or indeed imply any existential proposition at all ; it merely asserts a hypothetical correlation between stimulus and sensation, whenever and wherever they may occur. And this may be held to apply to all the other general propositions that go to constitute a system of psychology. As for their justification, it may be argued that sufficient inductive evidence can be found by the psychologist in his own experience. There remains, however, the difficulty that if the assumption that other people have experiences, which are analogous to his own but inaccessible to his observation, is for him devoid of meaning, then, in applying his laws to other people, he will have to interpret them as asserting correlations of behaviour such as he can in principle observe ; and this means that even if he can regard these laws as being true of other people, it will not be in the same sense as they are true of himself. This asymmetry is indeed removed if one extends the behaviouristic interpretation to propositions about one's own experiences also. But this is a proposal that I have already found reason to reject.[1]

However, even if it could be shown that the assumption that other people have experiences in the same sense as one has oneself was not required either by the physical or the mental sciences, this would not prove that one was not entitled to make it ; and indeed the rejection of it, on the ground that it is not a significant hypothesis, seems paradoxical at the least. This would not indeed be a fatal objection if the argument which led to its rejection were sound ; but I do not now think that it is. The principle on which the argument is founded is that I cannot significantly assert the existence of anything that I could not conceivably observe. But to

[1] Pp. 149-51.

determine the force of this principle it is necessary first to discover what is implied here by the use of the word " I ".[1] Consider, for example, the application of the principle to propositions about the past. It might be argued that since I cannot now observe any past events, I can only attach meaning to propositions which seem to refer to the past if I interpret them as referring to a set of experiences which I could obtain now, or in the future, these experiences being such as would ordinarily be regarded as indirect evidence for the truth of the propositions in question.[2] But this would be a mistake. For if it is to be said that the limits of my understanding of empirical propositions are coextensive with the limits of my observation, the field of my possible observations must not be held to be restricted by the contingent fact that I am a person who happens to be living at a particular time, any more than it is restricted by the contingent fact that I happen at any given moment to occupy a particular position in space. Just as it is possible, in principle, that I should be making observations which I cannot actually make because I do not happen to be situated in the requisite position in space, so is it possible, in principle, that I should be making observations which I cannot actually make because I do not happen to be situated in the requisite position in time. And from this it follows that it is not necessary for the apparent temporal

---

[1] In my development of this point I am indebted to Mr. G. Ryle. *Vide* his " Unverifiability by Me ", *Analysis*, 4.1.

[2] Cf. C. I. Lewis, *Mind and the World Order*, pp. 150-53. This was formerly my own view also.

reference of propositions about the past to be distorted in order that they should be capable of being understood.

Now the question is whether there is any essential difference, with respect to our present problem, between this case and the case of propositions about other people's experiences. It may be suggested that there is, on the ground that whereas it is a contingent fact that I am living at a particular date and so am unable to observe events which occurred at an earlier date, it is a necessary fact that I cannot have anybody else's experiences. But I do not think that this does make an essential difference. For although it is a necessary fact that the series of experiences that constitutes my history does not in any way overlap with the series of experiences that constitutes the history of any other person, inasmuch as we do not at present choose to attach any meaning to statements that would imply the intersection of such series, nevertheless, with regard to any given experience, it is a contingent fact that it belongs to one series rather than another. And for this reason I have no difficulty in conceiving that there may be experiences which are not related to my experiences in the ways that would be required to constitute them elements in my empirical history, but are related in similar ways to one another. The contents of these experiences do indeed fall outside the scope of my observation, inasmuch as they form part of a different series from that which constitutes the person that I happen to be, but this does not

mean that my references to them are " unverifiable "
in the sense that statements about transcendent
objects are. For whereas it is logically inconceivable
that I should observe a transcendent object, inasmuch as it is by definition beyond the limits of all
possible experience, it is not logically inconceivable
that I should have an experience that is in fact
owned by someone else. This does not mean that
any experience can actually be both mine and someone else's ; for I have shown that that possibility is
ruled out by the conventions of our language. It
means only that with regard to any experience that is
in fact the experience of a person other than myself,
it is conceivable that it should have been not his
but mine. The point is that there is nothing in an
experience considered by itself, apart from the relations that it happens to bear to other phenomena, to
make it form part of one person's history rather than
another's. And so I think it may be concluded that
the sense in which the experiences of other persons
are inaccessible to my observation is not such as to
make the hypothesis of their existence inaccessible
to my understanding.

Once this *a priori* difficulty is removed, it becomes
possible to rely on analogical arguments to justify
beliefs about other people's experiences, the strongest
of these arguments being those that are made to
depend not upon a resemblance in the appearances
of one's own and other bodies, but upon one's
observation of what may be called purposive behaviour
on the part of others, and especially their use of

signs. And here I agree with Professor Price [1] that the greatest weight should be attached to the fact that other people use signs which may convey information not previously possessed by oneself. It is sometimes made an objection to arguments of this sort that our beliefs about other people's experiences are derived immediately from the evidence of their behaviour and do not in fact involve any such processes of reasoning as these arguments require. But this, though it may be true, is beside the point. For it is necessary to distinguish between the genesis of a belief and its justification; and my problem has been, not to give a psychological account of the way in which we arrive at such beliefs, but only to remove the difficulties that seem to stand in the way of their being justified.

[1] *Vide* " Our Evidence for the Existence of Other Minds ". *Philosophy*, October 1938.

IV

CAUSALITY AND PERCEPTION

16. THE CAUSAL THEORY OF PERCEPTION

IT will be remembered that the conclusion to which
I came as the result of my examination of the argument from illusion was that, while the argument did
not show that the position of a naïve realist must
necessarily involve him in any logical or factual error,
it did nevertheless provide us with an inducement
to define our terms in such a way as to exclude the
possibility of our being directly aware of material
things. There is, however, a danger in this procedure, in that the objects of which we now say that
we are directly aware may be thought to form a
barrier between " our minds " and the material
world ; and this danger is not entirely removed by
our exposing the confusion of thought which is evinced
by the attempt to locate these objects " in the mind ".
For the question that will be raised is how, if material
things, or whatever other real objects may be conceived to exist outside sense-data, are not directly
given, one can ever acquire any knowledge of them ;
and this question has to be met, whatever view one
takes of the status of sense-data themselves. The

usual answer has been that one can justify beliefs about the existence and character of things outside sense-data by means of a causal argument, and it is through accepting this answer that philosophers come to hold what is known as a causal theory of perception. I shall argue, however, that such a view is logically untenable and, consequently, that we must look elsewhere than to the causal theory of perception for a satisfactory account of our knowledge of the external world.

What I am calling the causal theory differs from the other philosophical theories of perception that I have mentioned in that it cannot be regarded merely as proposing the use of a special terminology for describing our perceptual experience. It may, however, be represented as being analogous to them to the extent that the questions with which it is concerned are linguistic rather than factual. On this showing, its purpose is to elucidate the meaning of sentences of the form " this is an *x* " and " *A* is perceptually conscious of *x* ", where *A* stands for a person and *x* for a material thing. And to this purpose it may give effect in various ways. Thus, the theory may be simply that " this is *x* " is equivalent to " this is caused by *x* ", or else that it is equivalent to " this is a member of a group, or ' family ',[1] of sense-data which are caused by *x* ". Alternatively, it may be held that " this is an *x* " is equivalent to " this is caused by *y* " or to " this is a member of a

---

[1] This is the word that Professor Price uses to collate the sense-data that " belong to the same material thing ". Cf. *Perception*, pp. 218-72.

group, or ' family ', of sense-data which are caused
by y ", where y stands for something that would not
ordinarily itself be called a material thing, such as a
" wave of probability " or a " volition of God ".
Similarly, in the case of the analysis of perceptual
consciousness, it may be held that "A is perceptually
conscious of x " is equivalent to "A is sensing a
sense-datum and inferring that it has x for its cause "
or to "A is sensing a sense-datum and inferring that
it belongs to a family of sense-data which have x
for their cause " ; or else some such phrase as
" taking for granted ", or " assuming in virtue
of past experience ", may be substituted for the
word " inferring " in one or other of these expressions, or y, as in the other case, for x. But it will
not be necessary to consider each of these possible
variants of the causal theory in detail. For the objection I shall subsequently bring forward holds equally
against them all. The essential point to bear in mind
is that, in every case, the object that is singled out
as the cause of what is immediately observed is not
itself supposed to be observable.

It is to be remarked that while those who adopt a
causal theory about the nature of perceptual consciousness are committed to holding a causal theory
about the analysis of propositions which imply the
presence of material things, the converse is not true.
There would be no logical inconsistency in saying,
for example, that whereas " this is x ", where x stood
for a material thing, meant " this is caused by x ",
"A is perceptually conscious of x " meant "A is

sensing a sense-datum and taking it to be part of the surface of x ". If anyone held this view, he would presumably wish to maintain that, given the sense-datum, it was possible to infer the existence of the material thing which was its cause ; but this would not imply that perceptual consciousness itself involved any such process of inference. And, in fact, it is generally agreed that it does not. It must, however, be admitted that a proposition of the form " this is x ", where x stands for a material thing, is usually intended to express the content of a perception ; so that if the percipient is not himself aware that he is making any causal inference, it follows either that such propositions are not to be analysed causally, or else that their meaning is different from what their authors suppose it to be. In support of the second alternative, it may be argued that it is not uncommon for a proposition to be found, on analysis, to have a complexity of meaning which is not explicitly recognized by many of those who use it. And indeed, if it could be shown that there were strong arguments in favour of a causal analysis of propositions asserting the presence of material things, I do not think that the fact that it did not appear to agree with what was unreflectingly assumed to be the meaning of such propositions would in itself be a sufficient reason for rejecting it.

The fact is, however, that while the causal theory of perception may be represented as a theory about the meaning of a certain class of propositions, it is not from considerations of meaning that philosophers have actually come to adopt it. They have assumed rather that the argument from illusion proves that it is false, as a matter of fact, that anyone ever directly observes a material thing ; and they have then had recourse to a causal theory as the only means of accounting for the knowledge of the existence and behaviour of material things, which they did not doubt that they possessed. The important feature of this procedure is that it rests upon the assumption that the character of our sense-data, or whatever objects it is held that we do directly observe, gives us good reason to believe that they are dependent upon external causes. And it is in this assumption, whether it takes the form of discovering these causes in material things, as they are conceived by common sense, or, what is now more fashionable, in scientific objects, such as atoms and electrons, or, as in Berkeley's philosophy, in the activities of a God, that the main interest of the causal theory lies. It is possible indeed both to deny this assumption and still to adhere to a causal analysis of propositions asserting the presence of material things, if one is prepared, as Hume apparently was, to draw the conclusion that one's beliefs in the existence of material things are altogether unjustifiable. But such a procedure would be reasonable only if there were good grounds, independently of any argument that involved this assumption, for supposing that the meaning of such propositions was correctly rendered by some form of the causal theory. And this does not appear to be the case.

The argument that is supposed to justify this postulation of external causes proceeds by the following stages. It is maintained, first, that every event has a cause; secondly, that sense-data are events; thirdly, that one's sense-data are not, for the most part, caused by one's own volitions or by any other of one's own conscious mental activities or states; and fourthly, that they are not caused by one another. From these premises it is deduced that they must, for the most part, have causes that one cannot directly observe; and then an attempt may be made to show how the specific character and behaviour of these external causes may be inferred from the character of one's sense-data. Up to this final step, the argument is substantially the same for all versions of the theory. The differences between them relate only to the nature of these external causes and the degree to which they can be known. The most common assumption has been that one is justified in ascribing to them at any rate the primary qualities of extension, figure, solidity, number and motion; and ingenious methods have been devised by means of which one is supposed to be able to discover by what determinate forms of these qualities they are characterized on particular occasions.[1] But there is no point in my discussing the validity of these methods before I have settled the question whether there is any reason to believe in the existence of any such external causes at all. For if it turns out that there is no reason to believe in their existence,

---

[1] Cf. H. H. Price, *Perception*, pp. 74-99.

the question of the means by which one is to ascertain their specific character will not arise.

I may now begin by admitting the validity of the second and third stages of the argument I have just set forth. It is true that I have been speaking of sense-data as " objects " rather than " events ". But to every sense-datum, conceived as an object, there corresponds the event of its occurrence ; and the statements that are made about sense-data as objects could all be expressed in terms of these events. Such propositions, for example, as that I am simultaneously sensing a blue and a white visual sense-datum, or that I am sensing auditory sense-data which are fainter than those that I was sensing a moment ago, could also be expressed by saying that there is a simultaneous occurrence of a blue and a white sense-datum in my visual sense-field, or that there are occurrences in my auditory sense-field of sense-data which are fainter than those that occurred in its predecessor. And on this basis it is possible to effect a general transition from the terminology of sense-data, as objects, to the terminology of sensible events. The statement that sense-data are events may accordingly be accepted, not as a factual proposition, but as a proposal to use the "event" terminology, at any rate for the elaboration of the causal theory.

With regard to the proposition that the causes of our sense-data are not, in general, to be found in our own conscious mental activities or states, a certain amount of explanation is required to show that one is justified in conceding it. One needs here to follow the example of Professor Price, who draws a distinction between what he calls the " standing " and the " differential conditions " of a sense-datum. The standing conditions, he explains, are those that " condition *all* the sense-data of any one sense " ; a differential condition is one that " accounts for the difference " between one such sense-datum and another, say between " this red sense-datum and that blue one, between this square one and that elliptical one ". And he argues, with justice, that those who speak loosely of the cause of a sense-datum, as if it had only a single cause, must be understood in this context to be referring to its differential condition.[1] Thus, the view of those who maintain that the causes of our sense-data must, in most cases, lie " outside ourselves " is not that the psychological state of the observer may not be a permanent standing condition of his sense-data, but only that it is not, in the ordinary way, a differential condition. In certain cases of complete hallucination it may indeed be possible to account for the occurrence of the deceptive sense-data by correlating them with psychological peculiarities of the observer ; but such cases are exceptional. There does not, in general, appear to be a regular correspondence between a person's sense-data and the series of his " mental " states. The changing course of his sense-history seems, for the most part, as if it were imposed upon him " from outside " ; it is not the product of his volition ; nor

---

[1] Cf. *Perception*, p. 70.

can it be systematically correlated with any course of psychological change " within himself ". This does not prevent the psychological state of an observer from being what I have called a standing condition of his sense-data, but it can legitimately be taken to prove that it is not a differential condition. And it is with the " causes " of sense-data, as differential conditions, that the exponents of causal theories of perception are primarily concerned.

We come then to the point that if it is true that every event has a cause, and, consequently, that there is a cause of the occurrence of every sense-datum, the possibilities before us are either that the sense-data for which there is no differential condition to be found in the psychological state of the observer are caused by one another, or else that they have external causes. But is it, in fact, the case that every event has a cause ? What meaning indeed are we to give to the statement that one event is the cause of another ? These are the main questions that I must now attempt to answer.

17. Formulation of " the Principle of Determinism "

The proposition that every event has a cause is sometimes referred to as the principle of determinism. And this principle of determinism may, perhaps, be re-expressed, in a form suggested by Jean Nicod, by saying that every event e of a kind E is a case of an event of some other kind, every instance of which is a case of an instance of E.[1] In this formula, the expression " is a case of " is intended to imply no more than that if an event of the one kind occurs an event of the other kind occurs also. It carries no implication as to the temporal order of the two events, so that if one desires to bring the formula into accordance with the ordinary conception of causality, one will have to add to it a proviso that the event of which e is a case is temporally prior to or, perhaps, simultaneous with e. For, as the words " cause " and " effect " are ordinarily understood, it is impossible for the effect to precede the cause ; and not everybody would allow that they could even be simultaneous. It has, indeed, been argued that this is a superstition, and that there can be no reason *a priori* for denying that " the future ' determines ' the past in exactly the same sense in which the past ' determines ' the future ".[2] But the answer is that the terms " cause " and " effect " are in fact applied in such a way as to exclude this possibility *a priori*. All the same, it can legitimately be argued that this way of applying these terms marks a distinction that is of no theoretical importance, so that it would be advisable to refashion them in a way that would remove this temporal restriction. And with this suggestion I shall find reason to agree.

---

[1] *Foundations of Geometry and Induction* (translated by P. P. Wiener), p. 223. Nicod formulates his principle in terms of the relationship of " characters " rather than " events " : but this is only a terminological difference.

[2] Bertrand Russell, " On the Notion of Cause ", *Mysticism and Logic*, p. 195.

Another point in which our formula is somewhat at variance with popular notions of causality is that it does not differentiate between a " cause " and the accompanying " conditions ", the presence of which is thought to be necessary for the cause to produce its effect. And the reason for this is that while this use of a special name to refer to one among a number of " jointly sufficient conditions " may serve to single out an event as one in which the speaker is particularly interested, it does not correspond to any difference of function with regard to the production of the effect. Accordingly, the event by which a given event e is determined is always to be understood, in our formula, as comprising the whole set of conditions of which it is true, in the case in question, both that they are jointly sufficient for the occurrence of e, and that no sub-set of them is also sufficient. It might indeed be more accurate to refer to this " determinant " as a class of events. But the description of it as a single event is convenient for the purposes of exposition and is not, in this context, likely to be misleading.

It must also be noticed that the formula allows for what is known as the plurality of causes. If an event e of the kind E is a case of another event c of the kind C, it follows, taking c to be the determinant, that every event of the kind C is a case of some event of the kind E, but not that every event of the kind E is a case of some event of the kind C. A second event e^1, which is also of the kind E, may be a case, not of any event of the kind C, but of some event of the kind D, where again it is true that every instance of D is a case of some instance of E, but not true that every instance of E is a case of some instance of D. If one wishes to rule out this possibility of the plurality of causes one must emend the formula so as to make it imply not merely that every instance of E is a case of an instance of some other kind of event, every instance of which is a case of an instance of E, but also that this second kind of event is the same for all instances of E. That is to say, taking c to be the determinant on a particular occasion, one must assert, not only that all instances of C are cases of instances of E, but also that all instances of E are cases of instances of C. Thus, as I have formulated them, the relation between the principle of determinism which allows for, and that which excludes, the possibility of the plurality of causes is that the second entails the first but is not entailed by it. In other words, the first makes a smaller claim than the second, and should therefore be easier to establish. It does not, indeed, imply that the plurality of causes actually obtains in nature, but it does leave this possibility open. And since we have no ground for refusing to entertain this possibility, the weaker form of the principle of determinism may, at any rate at this stage of our discussion, legitimately be preferred.

The main objection that is likely to be raised against this re-formulation of the proposition that every event has a cause is that by making its validity a matter of there being universal *de facto* conjunctions between events of different kinds, I fail to take into account the necessity of the connexion which is supposed to obtain between cause and effect. But the reason why I do not take it into account is simply that this idea of necessary connexion has no counterpart at all in the observable facts. No doubt the use of the word " cause " does to most minds vaguely convey a suggestion that events in some way compel one another to occur. But this, as I shall try to show, is the legacy of a discarded metaphysic which can survive in a " scientific " concept only as a more or less misleading metaphor. It may indeed be held that by ridding it of this implication, I transform the meaning of " causality " to such an extent as to make the retention of the word excessively misleading. But this is a question of verbal expediency with which I am not at present concerned. For what I am now going to attempt is first to dispose satisfactorily of " the idea of necessary connexion ", and then to consider how far belief in the principle of determinism, when it is understood in the sense that I have outlined, is justified by the empirical facts.

18. The Animistic Idea of Necessary Connexion

It was recognized by Hume that " when we look about us towards external objects, and consider the operations of causes, we are never able, in a single instance, to discover any power or necessary connexion ; any quality which binds the effect to the cause, and renders the one an infallible consequence of the other ".[1] And from this he concluded that the idea of necessary connexion, which must, so he thought, somehow be derived from experience, was not a copy of any " impression of the outward senses ". Nor could he trace it to any single " internal impression " ; not even to our consciousness of the influence of the will. For while we are frequently aware that " the motion of our body follows upon the command of our will ", we are not conscious of any " power or force " which connects the event constituted by an act of willing with its physical consequent ; nor are ever in a position to be able to predict with certainty that an act of willing will have its designed result. And the same arguments hold against the view that our idea of necessary connexion is derived from a consciousness of a " power or energy in our own minds when, by an act or command of our will, we raise up a new idea ". Hume's own solution is that " the idea of necessary connexion among events arises from a number of similar instances which occur of the constant conjunction of these events ". " There is ", he says, " nothing in a number of instances different from any single instance, which is supposed to be exactly similar, except only that after a repetition of similar instances the mind is carried by habit, upon the appearance of an event, to expect its usual attendant, and to believe that it will exist. This connexion,

[1] *An Enquiry concerning Human Understanding*, Part I, section vii.

therefore, which we *feel* in the mind, this customary transition of the imagination from an object to its usual attendant, is the sentiment or impression from which we form the idea of power or necessary connexion." If we are able to derive from a number of instances of the conjunction of two different sorts of events this idea of necessary connexion which we cannot derive from any single instance, it is not, on this view, because of any new factor that the multiplication of instances introduces into the events themselves. The reason is simply that when a man has observed several instances of this kind " he *feels* the events to be *connected* in his imagination, and can readily foretell the existence of one from the appearance of the other. When we say therefore that one object is connected with another we mean only that they have acquired a connexion in our thought, and give rise to this inference, by which they become proofs of each other's existence."

Now if our purpose were to give to the expression " necessary connexion " a meaning that would be substantially in accordance with ordinary usage, but would, at the same time, make it refer only to what was capable of being observed, Hume's theory could, with certain slight modifications, be regarded as acceptable. But if the theory is designed, as seems to be the case, to account for the origin of the belief that there attaches to the events themselves a quality or relation " which binds the effect to the cause", it is plainly inadequate. It may perhaps explain how we pass from the recognition that in all the cases, hitherto observed, events of the kind *A* have been succeeded by events of the kind *B*, to a belief that they are, in fact, conjoined in all cases ; but it does not at all account for the assumption that instances of *B must* always follow instances of *A*, as distinct from the assumption that they actually always have, and always will. How then are we to explain this use of the word " must " ? The answer is, I think, that it is either a relic of animism, or else reveals an inclination to treat causal connexion as if it were a form of logical necessity. These two explanations are not, indeed, psychologically exclusive of one another. It is arguable, for instance, that the attempt to assimilate causality to logical entailment is, on the part of some philosophers, a rationalization of an unconscious animistic belief in " necessary connexion ". But they are at any rate logically distinct ; and it will be convenient to deal with them separately.

To say that a belief is animistic, in its origin or implications, is not always to say that it is erroneous. Let it be granted, for the sake of argument, that what we ascribe to things, when we say that they act causally upon one another, is something analogous to " what we experience in our own doing and enduring ".[1] Then, to one who is not an animist, it will seem to follow that most causal propositions are false. For most of them ascribe causal properties to things which are, so he will argue, incapable of acting or suffering in the way that human beings act and

[1] *Vide* G. F. Stout, *Mind and Matter*, p. 10.

suffer. But suppose that one does not start with the premise that animism is false. In that case, the adoption of this view of causality may lead one to conclude, not that it is a mistake to ascribe causal properties to material things, but rather that, inasmuch as they undoubtedly possess causal properties, these things are not altogether inanimate. And this is, in fact, a view that has recently been put forward by Professor G. F. Stout. He maintains that if one accepts a Humean analysis of the evidence which there is for believing that events of different kinds are causally related, then one can have no valid ground for attaching even the slightest probability to any supposed causal law. To fill the " logical gap which would otherwise destroy the validity of causal inference ",[1] it is necessary, in his opinion, to bring in the notion of " active tendency ", with which he holds that we are made familiar by our experience of our own conative states. The illustration that he gives to show how he would make use of this notion is that of a stretched bow. " We say that there is a tendency for the bow to unbend." And this use of the word " tendency " does not, so he maintains, " merely represent the hypothetical proposition, *if the archer removes his fingers, the bow will as a matter of fact unbend* ".[1] For he argues that if it is interpreted in this way, " there is no reason in the nature of this initial situation why, when the archer removes his hand, it should change at all, or, if it does so, why it should change in one way rather than in any one of an infinity of alternative ways which are also geometrically possible ".[1] His own interpretation, which he puts forward as escaping this objection, is that " the initial situation is such that the bow is actually tending to unbend, so that when the pressure of the archer's hand is removed this tendency is released and, so far as other conditions permit, fulfils itself ".[1] " This tendency ", he says, " actually exists before it is fulfilled, and would exist even if it were never fulfilled at all. It is actual in the same sense in which the process of unbending is actual when it takes place." [1] He does not go so far as to infer from this that the bow, and all the other material things to which he attributes " active tendencies " on the ground that they have causal properties, are themselves animate in the way that human beings are animate ; but he does infer that they are somehow controlled by a mind. The kind of tendency that they are supposed to exhibit is what he calls " secondary tendency ". " It is active tendency only so far as it is a partial factor in the total process in which primary tendency moves towards its own fulfilment or defeat." [2] But, as such, it is taken to presuppose, in every case, the existence of a primary tendency. And so Professor Stout arrives at the conclusion that " it is required that mind shall through and through enter into the constitution of nature ".[3]

---

[1] *Ibid.*   [2] *Mind and Matter*, p. 29.
[3] *Ibid.* p. 135

Reviewing this argument, I find that it depends entirely upon two assumptions. The first is that there actually are occasions on which we are justified in making causal inferences. The second is that we should not be so justified unless we were capable of apprehending that the things to which we ascribed causal properties were possessed of active tendencies, in this literal sense. Apart from these assumptions there is no ground at all for supposing that material things can ever truly be said to be active, except by way of metaphor. To return to the example of the stretched bow, it must surely be admitted that all that can ever be observed in such a case is, first, that the various parts of the bow stand in a certain spatial relationship to each other, and then, that this relationship is altered, when the archer's fingers are removed. To read into the initial situation the presence of a " real tendency " in the bow to unbend is, accordingly, to adopt a hypothesis that cannot in any way be verified. Nevertheless, argues Professor Stout, without hypotheses of this kind it is impossible to justify causal inference. But the answer to this is, first, that this demand for the justification of causal inference is itself unwarrantable; and, secondly, that even if such a justification were required, the assumption of active tendencies would not provide it.

The demand is unwarrantable because it involves the application to inductive reasoning of a standard of rationality that is appropriate to deductive reasoning only. If one means by " having a good reason " for believing that a particular event will occur, that

one knows for certain a proposition, or set of propositions, from which the proposition describing the
occurrence of the event can be formally deduced,
then, I think, it must be said that, in fact, one never
has a good reason for believing that any event will
occur, rather than any other. For, whatever it is
that one may happen to be observing at any given
moment, the proposition which describes it will
always be logically compatible with any significant
assumption whatsoever concerning the nature of
what is to be observed at any other moment.
Admittedly, a proposition describing an " effect "
may be validly deduced from a conjunction of the
proposition describing the " cause " with a general
proposition which states that events of the relevant
kinds are causally connected ; and there may be
some other, more general, causal law from which this
general proposition can in its turn be validly deduced.
But the foundations upon which arguments of this
kind ultimately rest must always be propositions for
which the evidence is wholly inductive ; and for
believing these propositions there cannot be any
reason at all, in the sense in which there can be a
reason for believing the conclusion of a purely formal
argument. It does not follow, however, that when
we say, as we very often do, that certain causal
inferences are reasonable, we are invariably mistaken.
For the fact is that, in calling such inferences reasonable, we do not mean to claim that they are demonstrative. What we mean, when we say that we have
good reason to believe a proposition, which is not

formally demonstrable, is, I think, simply that it is supported by strong inductive evidence, or, in other words, that it accords with our past experience.[1] And if this is so, there is no sense in asking whether the accepted general procedure of arguing from observed to unobserved cases is itself reasonable; for in the application of the criteria by which we determine what is reasonable the validity of this procedure is already presupposed. I suggest, therefore, that the philosophers who make this demand for a " justification of induction " are succumbing, here again, to the fallacy of attempting to generalize a question that is significant only in relation to some particular case.

Returning now to the hypothesis of active tendencies, I maintain that, in any case, it fails to fulfil the purpose for which it is designed. For let us suppose, to recur to Professor Stout's example, that it is actually possible to observe in the bow a positive inclination to unbend. We shall still not be able formally to deduce from this either that the

---

[1] It is to be noted that this procedure does not require that our memory judgements, which supply the necessary information about the character of our past experience, shall themselves be *unquestionably* true. Judgements about the past are subject to the same criteria of " rationality " as judgements about the future. But our decision that a given judgement of memory is rational will always involve our assuming the validity of some other memory judgements. And while the rationality of this assumption can be tested in its turn, this test will itself involve a further assumption of a similar kind ; and this is a process that can be continued indefinitely. It follows that the question whether it is rational for us to trust our memories is yet another instance of the kind of question that is significant with respect to particular cases, but cannot be significantly generalized.

bow will in fact unbend, or even, in the event of its unbending, that it would not have unbent if this inclination had been absent. That is to say, it cannot be demonstrated that the existence of the tendency is either a sufficient, or even an indispensable condition of the occurrence of the event, of which it is supposed to be a cause. So long as the word " tendency " is taken, as it must here be taken, not as a covert reference to what will subsequently happen, but only as a description of what is actually present, all that is effected by Professor Stout's hypothesis is the introducing of a greater complexity into the initial situation. It does not at all remove the impossibility of making a valid deductive inference from the existence of one situation to the existence of another. This point is important, since it is often urged as an objection to Hume that he misconceived the initial situation by treating a cause and its effect as two distinct events. What we observe, it is said, in the case of a particular causal sequence, is not just two separate events in a relation of spatio-temporal contiguity, but a unified complex ; we observe that one event is, as it were, " glued " to the other ; and it is suggested that this gives us reason to believe that the connexion is necessary and universal. Now, for my part, I have never observed this peculiar linking of events, and I am disposed to doubt whether anyone else has ever, in fact, succeeded in observing it. But the point is that, even if it were observable, this would not in any way diminish the force of Hume's contention that we cannot have demonstrative knowledge that any proposition, affirming a " causal law ", will hold good for other instances than those from which it was actually derived. To make this clear, let us represent the " link " by the relation-symbol R. Then, it may be said that the sort of observation on which we seek to base our causal law is observation, not merely of an event a succeeded by an event b, but of the unified complex aRb. But would this give us any more reason to believe in the validity of any general proposition connecting events of the kind A with events of the kind B ? It is easy to see that it would not. For, just as it is impossible to deduce, from the observation of particular instances of A followed by instances of B, that all instances of A are followed by instances of B, or even that any single further instance of A will be followed by an instance of B, so would it be impossible to deduce, from the observation of particular instances of the complex aRb, either that all instances of A had the property Rb, or even that any single further instance would have it. It is true that one could always make sure that any instance of A should have the property Rb by translating the " causal law " in question into an *a priori* proposition ; it would simply be a matter of refusing to call anything that lacked this property an instance of A. But this cannot be counted as an argument in favour of the assumption of the " link ", since this method could be used equally well to prove that every instance of A must just be followed by an instance of B. And, in any case, the scope of our knowledge cannot really be increased by devices of this sort. For the questions which may appear to be settled in this way, by a suitable choice of definitions, can always still be raised in other forms. Thus, in my example, it will still be possible to ask whether anything that is known to have all the properties that would, by definition, make it an instance of A, except the property of being followed by, or having the relation R to, an instance of B, really is a genuine instance of A ; and to this there will be no logically certain answer. We may define terms as we please ; but there is no escaping the fact that from a proposition that merely describes what one observes on a particular occasion, one cannot formally deduce any proposition whatsoever that implies the existence of anything else. And this will remain true, whatever view may be taken of the nature of what one actually observes.

From what I have said it should by now be clear that Hume was right to maintain that the impression of " force " or " effort " which a person may derive from his awareness of his own conative states does not exemplify the " idea of necessary connexion ", if this idea is understood to imply that in a causal sequence one event inevitably follows the other. For not only is it impossible, as Hume himself remarked, to deduce, from the single premise that one has the experience of willing, that the result which is intended will actually come about, but, even in the case in which the expected result does actually ensue, it still cannot be demonstrated that the act of willing was indispensable to its occurrence ; it is impossible, with the premises available, to prove deductively that the event would not have occurred just the same even if it had not been willed as it was. There is, indeed, one sense of the word " cause " in which it obviously does stand for something of which we have an " internal impression ". For, as Professor Collingwood has pointed out,[1] we sometimes use the word in such a way that " that which is caused is the free and deliberate act of a conscious agent, and ' causing ' him to do it means affording him a motive for doing it ". And this, according to Collingwood, is historically the earliest of the senses in which the word is currently used, and is still the only " proper " sense. But it is clear that in the situations to which the word can be applied, in this usage, there is nothing whatsoever to give rise to the idea of necessary connexion ; and indeed it is hard to see how this idea could ever have arisen as part of an animistic theory which consisted merely in the false attribution to inanimate objects of properties that were exclusively characteristic of human beings. To explain its origin animistically, I think we must have recourse, not to anything that people actually experience, in their relations to one another or to the material world, but rather to a primitive superstition, according to which external things are incorporated with human beings into a society whose laws are prescribed and enforced by supernatural agency.

[1] In his paper " On the So-called Idea of Causation ", *Proceedings of the Aristotelian Society*, 1937–8.

For I think that it is only by making it a consequence of the metaphysical hypothesis that the order of events is supernaturally determined that we are able to account for the attribution of " necessity " to the supposedly empirical relation between cause and effect.

In this connexion I have been interested to read, in an article by Dr. Hans Kelsen which is devoted to a discussion of this problem,[1] that among primitive peoples, and also among the early Greek philosophers, it was customary to think of the order that was supposed to be supernaturally enforced upon the world as being essentially a moral order. And this suggests that the original significance of the word " must ", as it occurs in the statement that a given effect *must* follow a given cause, is not factual but normative. The " laws of nature " are conceived as projections of the moral and political laws of human society, and as being inviolable because they are expressions of divine will. More specifically, Dr. Kelsen's thesis is that " the law of universal causation " has been derived, historically, from a universal principle of retribution. The underlying conception is that effect follows cause as reward or punishment follows a good or evil act ; and it is thought to follow necessarily, because these sanctions are supposed to be enforced by a deity which, whether personified or not, is all-powerful. And this explains why it has been thought essential that the cause should precede the effect. On

[1] " Die Entstehung des Kausalgesetzes aus dem Vergeltungs-prinzip ", *Erkenntnis* (now *The Journal of Unified Science*), Band viii.

a functional view of causality this seems to be an arbitrary stipulation. For if one assumes that there is, in fact, a universal correlation between two different sorts of events, it is possible to infer from an occurrence of an instance of either to an occurrence of an instance of the other, with equal validity, whatever may be their temporal relationship ; so that it seems legitimate to say that " the future ' determines ' the past in exactly the same sense in which the past ' determines ' the future ".[1] But the case is quite different if the effect is conceived as " retribution " for the cause, for it is an analytic proposition that the good or evil action for which one is rewarded or punished is temporally prior to the retribution that it receives. Furthermore, since it is a feature of " the principle of retribution ", not only that good must be repaid with good, and evil with evil, but that the amount of good or evil repaid must be proportionate to the amount of good or evil done, one is able, if Kelsen is right, to account for the strange, but widely-held, opinion that every effect must be qualitatively or quantitatively akin to its cause. It is this opinion that has been responsible, among other things, for the reluctance of philosophers to admit that minds and bodies may directly interact. For the ground of their objection is not that observation fails to reveal conjunctions between physical and mental events, but simply that they are too dissimilar to be capable of being causally related. The truth of this principle that the effect must be at any rate a

[1] Bertrand Russell, *loc. cit.*

" manifestation of the same supreme variable " [1] as
the cause is, presumably, for such philosophers a
matter of *a priori* convention ; and, if this is so, it
cannot, strictly speaking, be rejected as a superstition, in the ordinary sense. But the inclusion of
such a principle in the definition of " causality " can
fairly be condemned as being in no way justified by
the empirical facts.

It is, indeed, to be noted that the fact that a
belief can be shown to have a superstitious origin is
not itself a sufficient reason for condemning it.
And if, in substituting a wholly functional for the
still partly normative concept of causality, one decides to do away with the temporal and qualitative
restrictions that have served to limit the field of
possible causal relations, it is not because the postu-
lates in question are unintelligible, but because the
use of them has shown itself to be misleading and
practically inconvenient. But the position is quite
different when we come to the animistic idea of
necessary connexion. For this is not intelligible
when it is divorced from its proper historical context. Accordingly, the question which must be put to
those who speak as if there were necessity in nature is
whether they really mean to imply that the laws of
nature are normative rules, enforced by a divine will.
If they do not mean to imply this, their talk of necessity is at best an unfortunate metaphor. If they do
mean to imply it, then not only are they assigning
to what have been assumed to be " scientific " terms

---

[1] Cf. John Wisdom, *Mind and Matter*, ch. vi.

a meaning that is at variance with modern scientific usage ; but, what is far more serious, they are interpreting causal propositions in such a way that they can have no valid reason whatsoever for believing any of them to be true.

19. CRITICISM OF THE RATIONALIST INTERPRETATION OF CAUSAL LAWS

The argument of those who maintain that the cause necessitates the effect, in the sense that causal propositions express relations of logical entailment,[1] is of the same order as that which is used to support the hypothesis of " active tendencies ". The premise from which these " rationalists " start is, again, that causal inferences are often reasonable ; and they take this to imply that they are deductive inferences from ground to consequent ; for they hold that otherwise there would be no valid reason for trusting them. And here again, the answer is, first, that no form of inductive inference ever is, or could be, " reasonable " in the sense of being formally demonstrative, but that, as we have already seen, this does not mean that such inferences cannot be reasonable, in the sense in which this word is properly applicable to them ; and secondly, that even if there were a genuine difficulty about the justification of causal inference, the adoption of this hypothesis would in any case fail to meet it. For let it be supposed that I observe

[1] A good exposition of this view is given by Dr. A. C. Ewing in a paper called " A Defence of Causality ", *Proceedings of the Aristotelian Society*, 1932–3.

an event which I take to be of the nature A, and that the evidence of past observations is that events of this kind have always, under similar conditions, been succeeded by events of the nature X; and suppose, further, that I am in doubt whether this gives me any reason at all for believing that events of these kinds are universally conjoined, or even that they will be conjoined in this particular case. It may then be put to me that my difficulty is illusory, on the ground that the proposition that an instance of X will occur in these conditions is logically entailed by the proposition that the event I am observing is an instance of A. It may be said, for example, in the words of Mr. H. W. B. Joseph, that " if a thing a under conditions c produces a change x in a subject s, the way in which it acts must be regarded as a partial expression of what it is. It could only act differently if it *were* different. As long therefore as it is a, and stands related under conditions c to a subject that is s, no other effect than x can be produced ; and to say that the same thing acting on the same thing under the same conditions may yet produce a different effect, is to say that a thing need not be what it is." " But this ", continues Mr. Joseph, " is in flat conflict with the Law of Identity. A thing, to be at all, must be something and can only be what it is. To assert a causal connexion between a and x implies that a acts as it does because it is what it is ; because, in fact, it is a. So long therefore as it is a, it must act thus ; and to assert that it may act otherwise on a subsequent occasion is to assert that

what is *a* is something other than the *a* which it is
declared to be." [1] Now if I accept this argument,
translating it into my terminology of events, I can
no longer have any doubt that if the event I am
observing really is an instance of *A* it will be
succeeded under these conditions by an instance of
X ; but the trouble is that I must at the same time
become correspondingly more doubtful whether this
really is an instance of *A*. For the evidence which I
formerly took to be sufficient to establish the truth
of this existential proposition will *ex hypothesi* not
be sufficient to establish it, now that I have widened
the connotation of *A* by making it logically necessary
that every instance of *A* should, in the relevant
conditions, be conjoined with an instance of *X*.
Unless I already have reason to believe that every
instance of *A*, in the sense in which I previously
understood this term is, not logically but factually,
conjoined in conditions such as these with an instance
of *X*, I can have no reason to believe that this really
is an event of the kind *A*, in the revised sense. And
this illustrates the point, which I have already made,
that it is futile to attempt to solve the " problem of
induction " by treating all general propositions of
law as if they were logically necessary. For any
question that there may have been about the validity
of the general propositions can always still be raised
as a question about the validity of the existential
propositions by which, as a result of this procedure,
they will have been replaced.

[1] *An Introduction to Logic*, p. 408.

If, now, we are asked whether it is true that causal propositions express relations of logical entailment, our answer must be that it depends entirely upon how one chooses to construct one's language. From the passage that I have quoted from the work of Mr. Joseph, it can be inferred that, in the language that he uses, all causal expressions are treated as partial definitions of some general term. Indeed, his whole " argument " is nothing more than an elaborate explication of this fact. Now this is not, I think, the ordinary practice, which seems rather to consist in taking some such expressions to be definitive, but not all. But the proposal that we should make it our practice is at any rate worthy of consideration. If we were to do so, we should have a language in which all synthetic causal propositions would take the form of singular existentials. We should not then be able to express at all what we now express by making causal propositions apply synthetically to an infinite number of possible cases ; but this would be the only way in which we should be verbally impoverished. So long as we were content to refer only to the actual or possible occurrences of particular events, our resources of expression would be neither increased nor lessened. We should find, however, that it would not be possible for us, as it is at present, to abandon a " causal law " without making a change in our usage of words. There would, indeed, be nothing describable as " the abandonment of a causal law ", except the redefinition of some term. And since it is more inconvenient to have to be constantly altering the meaning of words than merely to discard a series of empirical hypotheses, it would not be profitable for us to adopt the practice of making all causal expressions definitive unless we had very good reason to believe that the concepts that were yielded by these definitions would continue to be applicable to the empirical facts ; and these reasons could only be inductive in character.   And so, the suggestion that causal propositions should be taken to express relations of logical entailment, which has been put forward by philosophers as a means of avoiding what they supposed to be the irrational processes of inductive reasoning, seems rather to imply an extreme, and perhaps excessive, confidence in their validity.

It is, however, to be remarked that the tendency to make general propositions of law analytic is actually revealed in modern science.   A typical example of this is to be found in the claim, put forward by Professor E. A. Milne, that physics can be made to attain " the status of a geometry ".[1]   This point of view has been attacked [2] on the ground that it involves the unwarrantable assumption that one can have purely *a priori* knowledge of the workings of nature ; and Milne himself invites this objection by taking the possibility of dealing with physics in the way that he proposes as evidence that " the universe is rational ".   But the fact is that the question whether

[1] *Vide* " On the Origin of Laws of Nature ", published in a supplement to *Nature*, June 1937.

[2] *E.g.* by Professor H. Dingle: *vide* " Modern Aristotelianism ", *Nature*, May 1937.

physics can be made to attain the status of a geometry has nothing directly to do with the character of the physical world, or even with the character of our knowledge of it. It is simply a matter of one's being able to organize the accepted laws of physics into a self-consistent deductive system, and then choosing to treat the premises of this system, not as propositions about matters of fact, but as implicit definitions. If this procedure is carried out, the general propositions of physics will indeed become " truths of reason ", in the sense in which the propositions of a system of logic are " truths of reason " ; for they will be the logical consequences of conventional definitions ; but it does not by any means follow from this that one can establish laws of nature *a priori*. For no one would say that a proposition expressed a law of nature merely because it was assigned a place in some self-consistent abstract system. What is required is that the system should be realized in nature, or, in other words, that it should be capable of being used to make successful inductive inferences from one natural occurrence to another ; and this is a fact that can be ascertained only by empirical observation, and not *a priori*. Let us suppose, however, that it can be empirically established that this formalized system of physics is realized in nature. There will still be no warrant for concluding that " the universe is rational ", unless one is using this phrase merely to record the discovery of a certain measure of uniformity in the course of our experience ; and in that case it is a

very misleading phrase to use. What Milne appears
to mean by saying that the universe is rational is that
" given the statement of *what is*, the laws obeyed can
be deduced by a process of inference ". But this
is merely to call attention to a tautology. For by
" what is " he means that which satisfies the axioms
of his system ; and it is analytically true that anything that satisfies the axioms of a self-consistent
deductive system will also satisfy the theorems. Nor
is he justified in regarding it as in any way less
" magical " that nature should realize a certain
abstract system than that it should obey certain
empirical laws. For, as I have shown, these are not
descriptions of two distinct characteristics of nature ;
they are merely alternative ways of describing the
same empirical facts.

In fairness to the scientists who hold views like
Professor Milne's, it should be remarked that they
do not, in practice, assume that the validity of
physical theories can be determined otherwise than
by the test of empirical verification. Indeed, Milne
himself has stated that " non-verifiable propositions
about the world of nature have no significant
content ".[1] But how then are we to account for his
asserting, as he does, that " it is possible to derive
the laws of dynamics rationally without recourse to
experience " ? It may be that he is simply confused
by the fact that it is possible always to transform
empirical hypotheses into *a priori* conventions ; but
it is more profitable to assume that he is here drawing

[1] *Relativity, Gravitation and World Structure*, p. 83.

a distinction between the way in which the laws of nature are validated, or, in other words, shown to have empirical application, and the way in which they are discovered. We may then take him to be claiming that for the discovery of these laws one need not have recourse to experience, even if one must for their validation. And this may be conceded, in so far as it is possible, logically, that a system that had a purely fanciful origin might subsequently turn out to be realized in fact. But in the case where the derived propositions are " the laws of dynamics ", is the origin of the system really so fanciful ? Surely those who construct it already have empirical knowledge of what it would be useful for its premises to entail ? And is not their selection of the premises to a large extent governed by this ? It is true, no doubt, that the procedure of science is rather, as Kant said,[1] to ask nature questions than to make random collections of empirical facts. But surely it is the character of our past experience that is mainly responsible for our questions being what they are. Moreover, however much " creativeness " a theory may display, its propositions are not usually designed at the outset to be regarded as *a priori* truths. It is only when the theory has been very strongly substantiated by empirical observations that the tendency arises to make it wholly analytic. Nor is it always desirable to carry out such processes of axiomatization, even where the relationship of the

[1] *Critique of Pure Reason*, Preface to 2nd edition, xiii (p. 20 of N. Kemp Smith's translation).

propositions in question is such as to make it logically possible. For it is not conducive to the development of a science to " sanctify " hypotheses, so long as a convincing proof is lacking that they are likely to remain adequate to our experience.

20. Evaluation of " the Principle of Determinism "

It appears then that the attempt to save the " necessity " of causal relations by interpreting them as relations of logical entailment amounts, in the end to a plea for the extension of conventionalism in science, to a degree that goes beyond what is either customary or useful. In such a view there is no place at all for any principle of determinism, conceived as a hypothesis referring to the conjunction of logically distinct events. And, conversely, I have shown that there is no place in any such hypothesis for an " idea of necessary connexion ". I may, therefore, revert to my original formulation of the principle, as a proposition stating that every event e of a kind E is a case of an event of some other kind, every instance of which is a case of an instance of E. And the question I have now to consider is whether there is any good reason for believing that this proposition is true.

The validity of any such principle of determinism has often been disputed by philosophers, but usually, I think, for the wrong reasons. For the main objections that have been brought against it are that it is incompatible with the occurrence of miracles, and, more seriously, that it is incompatible with the freedom of the will ; and to these there has recently been added the further objection that physicists themselves have discarded it in favour of a " principle of indeterminacy ". But all these objections are based upon misunderstandings of the issues involved. Indeed, that the first two should be thought to raise any problems at all in this connexion can be taken only as a further sign that the concept of determinism has not yet been wholly freed from its theological associations. For, while those who regard the laws of nature as divine decrees may well think it necessary to consider whether their author might not choose to suspend their operations, or whether he allowed one to enjoy a measure of independence under his sovereignty, these are not questions that have any bearing upon the scope of determinism, as I understand it. Once we have abandoned this metaphysical conception of natural law in favour of one that is empirically significant, there is no reason why we should draw any distinction between the occurrence of a " miracle " and the occurrence of any other event that runs counter to some accepted hypothesis. Whether such events as are commonly designated as miracles have ever actually occurred is a question into which there is here no need to enter. For, even if they did occur, their occurrence would prove, not that the operation of the relevant laws could be suspended by a " higher power ", but simply that we were wrong in supposing them to be universal laws ; and then we should be left with the task of trying to find some other laws to put in their place. At present there seems, for example, to be no good reason to correlate the disappearance of physical deformities with the phenomena of religious ecstasy. But *a priori* this hypothesis is as legitimate as any other ; and, no doubt, if " cures " of this kind were common and well attested, we should find it expedient to revise our conception of medical science. But even so it would always come down to a belief in the *de facto* concomitance of the members of one class of empirical phenomena with those of another.

As for the freedom of the will, there does appear to be a difficulty in reconciling one's inclination to praise or blame people for their actions with the belief that these actions have been even partly determined by circumstances for which the agents are not themselves responsible. But this does not imply that for an action to be free its occurrence must be incapable of being brought under any natural law. On the contrary, an action would not ordinarily be said to be free at all in the sense which is here in question, unless its occurrence stood in some causal relation, at any rate to some preceding events in the personal history of the agent ; for it is held that if a man acts freely, in this sense, he is morally accountable for what he does ; and a man would not be said to be morally accountable for actions that were spontaneous in the sense of being completely uncaused. It has, indeed, been argued that one would not be justified in exacting retribution from a person on account of his actions unless he were, not merely immediately, but also ultimately responsible for them, in the sense that " each decision was due to an either infinite or world-long series of determinations of the will by the will " ; and this has been taken to show that anyone who is a moral agent must have existed for perhaps an infinite time before his birth.[1] But rather than adopt such a hypothesis, for which I cannot find any empirical evidence whatsoever, I should prefer to abandon the moral principle of retribution, for which in any case I feel a certain moral distaste. Moreover, the usual practice is not, I believe, to require that a person should be ultimately responsible for his actions, in any such sense as this, in order to be deserving of praise or blame, but rather to hold that he acts freely, and so is morally accountable, if his desire for an end to be achieved through the action is a causal factor in its occurrence, no matter what the other factors may be, and no matter how this desire itself may have been caused. At the same time, there is a tendency to " make allowances " for people which is strengthened by the belief that their decisions depend to a large extent upon factors " outside their control " ; and this may lead, perhaps, to a revision of the concept of " moral responsibility ". But this is purely a matter of the standardizing of a moral attitude ; and the fact that one may desire it settled in one way rather than another is not a

[1] Cf. John Wisdom, *Mind and Matter*, ch. viii.

premise from which anything at all can be inferred concerning the validity of causal laws.

In dealing with the so-called " principle of uncertainty " or " indeterminacy ", it is important not to make the mistake which Professor Stebbing has described as that of " supposing that the uncertainty relations show that there is anything indeterminate in Nature, or that science has now had to become inaccurate ".[1] For what this principle refers to is not an absence of order in sensible occurrences themselves, but the inadequacy of the conceptual scheme into which classical physicists have attempted to fit them. In classical physics, it makes sense to say of a particle that it has at any given time a definite position and a definite velocity ; it is assumed that these can be conjointly known, and that, given knowledge of the relative positions and velocities of a system of particles at any one moment, it is possible, by means of " deterministic laws ", to calculate precisely what would be their relative positions and velocities at any other moment. But in quantum physics none of this holds. In quantum physics there is not assumed to be any such thing as precise knowledge of the position and velocity of a particle at any single moment. There is a process which is described as that of ascertaining the position of an electron, but this has a consequence which is described as that of altering its velocity ; and, conversely, the process of ascertaining the velocity has, as its consequence, the alteration of the position ;

---

[1] *Philosophy and the Physicists*, p. 183.

and the more accurately either of these is measured, the greater becomes the uncertainty with respect to the other. It follows that the position and velocity of an electron at a given moment is not something that can be ascertained with precision ; it is said to be ascertainable only with a degree of uncertainty, to which a numerical value has been given in terms of Planck's constant h. But since " the position of an electron " and " its velocity " are expressions that have to be understood in terms of the operations by which these things are said to be measured, the proper inference to be drawn from this is not that the instruments of measurement are defective, still less, as sometimes seems to be suggested, that there is uncertainty in the particles themselves as to where they are or how fast they are going, but rather that in quantum physics it does not make sense to say of a particle that it simultaneously has a definite position and a definite velocity. In other words, the concept of a definite " initial state " of a system, as involving the assignment of precise values to the positions and velocities of its constituent particles, which was contained in the classical scheme of deterministic laws, is one that quantum physicists have discarded. Furthermore, when it comes to dealing with the phenomena which are described in quantum physics by saying that electrons jump from one orbit to another, it is not considered possible to discover laws that would enable one to predict the behaviour of any individual electron. The most that is allowed to be predictable is that a certain proportion of a group of electrons will behave in a given way. That is to say, the laws have become statistical in form instead of causal. There are statistical laws also in classical physics, as, for example, in the kinetic theory of gases ; but it was always thought that these were manifestations of underlying causal laws, which, if one knew enough about the particular details of the system in question, one would be able to discover. In quantum physics, on the other hand, the statistical laws are taken to be fundamental ; and I believe that most physicists now treat even the " causal laws " that seem to hold good in the macroscopic field as basically statistical. But this is just a way of saying that modern physicists have found it useful to give up employing a deterministic language. It may be that, by a radical revision of concepts, one could replace their terminology by one that would have the appearance of retaining determinism. But the only justification for doing this would be that the new terminology was the more convenient ; and there is no reason at present to suppose that this would be the case.

I have now explained in what sense it is correct to say that physicists no longer believe in determinism. But it is necessary to distinguish between a disbelief in the utility of deterministic concepts and a disbelief in the regularity of sensible occurrences. For the fact that it is found convenient not to assign determinism to the " entities of reason " which are postulated as a means of describing and predicting the course of sensible phenomena is not a proof that there cannot be universal correlations in the field of sensible phenomena themselves. At the same time, the fact that physicists have adopted the principle of indeterminacy, and the use of statistical in place of causal laws, does show that the " law of universal causation " is not, what many philosophers have taken it to be, a presupposition of science, and *a fortiori* that it is not a " necessity of thought ". For all that could reasonably be meant by calling it a presupposition of science is that scientists are bound to operate either with laws which are themselves causal, or with laws which, although they are themselves statistical, are assumed to rest upon a causal basis. And this has turned out not to be the case.

As for the view that the assumption of the law of universal causation is indispensable to human thought, there is abundant historical evidence against it, quite apart from the developments of modern science. Indeed, the account that I have already given of the origin of this assumption is itself an objection to such a view. For the primitive conception of nature as subject to a supernaturally regulated moral order is plainly not deterministic in any scientific sense. Nor can it be argued that, while it is possible for scientists to make successful use of an indeterministic language, it is necessary to conceive of the actual phenomena, with which the terms of such a language ultimately deal, as connected with each other by universal laws. For it is perfectly easy to imagine that there are kinds of sensible occurrences of which it is not true that any of them are related to any other kind of sensible occurrence in such a way that every instance of this second kind is a case of an instance of the kind in question. And indeed I believe this to be actually so.

To some philosophers this may appear to be objectionable, because it runs counter to Kant's dictum that the law of universal causation is a principle of the possibility of experience. But, in the first place, I cannot attach any significance to Kant's interpretation of this principle, since he speaks of causality as being both a synthetic and a necessary relation. And even if his conception of the law of universal causation were intelligible, he would still appear to have no reason for assigning to it the status that he does. The reason he actually gives is that " it is only in so far as our representations are necessitated in a certain order as regards their time-relations that they acquire objective meaning ",[1] and that " the rule, by which we determine something according to succession of time, is, that the condition under which an event invariably and necessarily follows is to be found in what precedes the event ".[2] For he argues that " the *objective relation* of appearances that follow upon one another is not to be determined through mere perception ",[3] on the ground that it is not legitimate to infer from a temporal succession in the order of one's apprehensions of appearances to a corresponding succession

[1] *Critique of Pure Reason :* The Second Analogy (p. 224 of N. Kemp Smith's translation).
[2] *Ibid.* (p. 226 of N. Kemp Smith's translation).
[3] *Ibid.* (p. 219 of N. Kemp Smith's translation)

in the objective temporal order of the appearances themselves. But while it is true that not every series of veridical sense-data is taken to be presentative of a series of temporally successive physical events, this does not prove at all that the " objective " temporal relationships of " appearances " are not to be determined through mere perception. The answer to Kant's question why the successive apprehensions of different parts of a house are not thought to be apprehensions of successive events, in the way that the successive apprehensions of the positions of a boat going downstream are,[1] is indeed that the former series is thought to be " reversible "[2] in a sense in which the latter is not. But all that this amounts to is that it is believed in the case of the house that from a different point of view a similar set of sense-data would have been obtainable in a different order, whereas in the case of the boat it is believed that the order of the sense-data would have been the same, whatever the point of view. And these beliefs refer exclusively to possible perceptions and are founded, not on any knowledge of " necessity " in either case, but simply upon past perceptual experience. The objective temporal order of events is determined principally by calculating, on the basis of one's own relevant sense-data and the reports of other observers, what series of perceptions would be obtainable, in conditions of observation which may or may not be actually realized. And this has

---

[1] *Critique of Pure Reason :* The Second Analogy (pp. 220-21 of N. Kemp Smith's translation).

[2] Cf. Part V, section 23 of this book.

nothing at all to do with any relation of " necessity ".

I conclude that if there is to be any reason for believing in the law of universal causation, as I have formulated it, it must be based upon our actual observations of the concurrences of sensible events. And indeed it has been argued that the number of universal laws which there are good inductive grounds for believing is sufficiently great to make it highly probable that every event is capable of being sub-sumed under some universal law, where what is understood by a " law " is not an analytic function, connecting one known event with another, but a hypothesis which can be successfully extrapolated. But is this actually the case ? Admittedly, there are a considerable number of well-attested laws which are thought to be universal and precise ; but they owe this appearance of precision to the fact that they are ex-pressed in terms which conceal the actual complexity of the phenomena involved. For when one attempts to restate a hypothesis referring to a conjunction of physical events as a hypothesis referring to a con-junction of sense-data, one finds that what is needed to establish the occurrence of one or other of the physical events is not the occurrence of a sense-datum of a single determinate kind, but merely that of any one out of a relatively indeterminate range of sense-data ; so that the precision of the hypothesis vanishes. And this applies even to the case of quantitative laws. Consider, for example, the case of a law of the form $z = ft$, the verification of which consists in showing that when t has a given numerical value x, z has the value y, where y is the appropriate function of x. In actual fact, the observations which are taken as verifying such a law are not simply observations of a pointer-reading y, but of pointer-readings that fall within the range of $y \pm e$, where e expresses the extent of what is called the " probable error ". And what the existence of this " probable error " must be taken to mean is not that one is allowing for a defect in the process of measurement, since there is no reason to suppose that the measurements that yield the value $y + e$ are any less correctly carried out than those that yield the precise value y, but rather that the law is not so exact in its application as its form would make it appear. Let us suppose, however, that difficulties of this kind can be removed by defining the term " sensible event " in such a way that all the sense-data that fall within a given range are understood to be instances of the same event. Even so, there remain many events the occurrence of which is not in fact inferrible by the use of established causal laws. In the first place, there are the events that are subsumed under statistical laws, where what is believed is not that every instance of C is a case of an instance of E, but only that a certain proportion of instances of C are cases of instances of E; and although it can always be hoped that these statistical laws will be found to be reducible to causal laws, there does not in many cases appear to be good empirical evidence for supposing that this hope will be fulfilled. And, secondly, there are the events whose occurrence is not, in the actual state of our knowledge, inferrible by any means at all. The determinist may answer that the fact that there are such events reveals only the measure of our ignorance ; and that " if one knew enough " one would be able to predict the course of one's experience in every detail. And no doubt it is through making an assumption of this kind that philosophers have come to deny the possibility of their being chance events, except in the sense in which the use of the word " chance " is taken merely as an expression of our ignorance of the actual cause. But if what is meant by the proviso that one should know enough is that one should know enough to be able to make the requisite inferences, then the statement that one could predict every occurrence if one knew enough is an idle tautology ; and if what is meant is that a closer study of the facts would actually provide us with the means of making these predictions, the statement begs the question at issue. For what I am maintaining is just that it is not very probable that every event is, in fact, connected with some other event, in such a way that one could infer its occurrence from the known occurrence of the other event by means of a valid causal, or even a valid statistical, " law ".

It seems to me, therefore, that there may very well be chance events, in the sense in which an event may properly be said to happen by chance when it is not true that it is conjoined with an instance of any other kind of event, all, or even most, instances of which are conjoined with instances of the same kind as itself. At the same time, it can never be demonstrated that any event is a chance event in this sense, since it is always conceivable that further investigation will reveal that events of its kind can after all be brought under some extrapolable law ; and perhaps " the law of universal causation " may be regarded as the expression of a resolve to try continually to narrow the field of what appear to be chance events. It then becomes a " heuristic maxim ", laying down an ideal of the complete explanation of phenomena, which may or may not be capable of being fulfilled.

21. The Causation of Sense-data

The point to which I must now draw attention is that whether this so-called law of universal causation is interpreted as a heuristic maxim, or as a not very probable statement of fact, my analysis has shown that the " causal relations " to which it refers must always be relations between events which are capable, at least in principle, of being observed. To attempt to make use of causal laws in order to infer from the occurrence of observed events to the existence of things that are outside the scope of any possible observation is not merely to put forward hypotheses for which there could not be any valid evidence ; it is to extend the use of the concept of causality beyond the field of its significant application. And it is this that constitutes the fatal objection to all forms of " the causal theory of perception " ; for it

is characteristic of all the theories that are commonly
brought under this heading that the causes of what
is actually observed are assumed themselves to be,
in principle, unobservable. In the case where the
external cause is conceived to be some state or action
of a transcendent God, the fallaciousness of this
reasoning is commonly recognized, at any rate by
philosophers. For they are generally willing to
agree with Kant that the causal argument for the
existence of God involves an unwarrantable extension
of the use of the concept of " causality ".[1] But it
does not appear to be so easily seen that exactly the
same fallacy is involved in the case where the
external cause is thought to be an unobservable
" physical object ". And the reason for this may
be that it is mistakenly believed that the assumption
of such external causes is a feature of contemporary
science, it being unfortunately the custom of many
scientists to speak as if scientific objects, such as
atoms and electrons, were constituents of a special
" world ". But the truth is not that the designations
of " sense-data ", " common-sense objects ", and
" scientific objects ", refer to constituents of different
" worlds ", which lie in some mysterious way
" beyond " one another, sense-data alone being
observable and the other " objects " inferrible as
their causes, but simply that these designations
belong to different languages, which are distinguished
from one another, not by referring to different sorts

[1] Cf. *Critique of Pure Reason* : " Impossibility of Cosmological
Proof of the Existence of God " (p. 511 of N. Kemp Smith's
translation).

H 2

of real objects, but by referring to phenomena in different ways. Thus, when Professor Eddington, for example, speaks of sitting down to write at his " two tables ", one of which " has extension, is comparatively permanent, is coloured, and above all is *substantial* ", while the other is " mostly emptiness ", being sparsely occupied by " numerous electric charges rushing about with great speed ",[1] he is using a metaphor which obscures instead of elucidating the nature of the facts. For all that he can properly mean is that in addition to being able to obtain the sense-data, the occurrence of which would justify his asserting that he was perceiving a table, in the everyday sense, he would also, in certain specifiable conditions, be able to obtain the sense-data, the occurrence of which is " explained " by scientists in terms of the movements of electric charges ; and there is nothing in this to warrant any metaphysical assertion about the reduplication of worlds.

What often leads to confusion in this context is an uncritical use of the word " reality ". Thus, it is sometimes said that what we take to be a solid, extended, coloured table is *really* only a scattered group of colourless electrons ; or it may be suggested that the familiar table alone is real, and the scientific table its " shadow " ; or else that both are real. But all that is at issue here is the choice of a verbal convention. It is simply a matter of specifying the

[1] *The Nature of the Physical World*, XI-XIII : quoted by L. S Stebbing in *Philosophy and the Physicists*, p. 55.

conditions in which it is to be said that a perception is veridical. So far as the phenomena themselves are concerned there is no ontological distinction to be drawn between the sense-data that one describes by referring to a table, in the ordinary sense, and those that one describes by referring to the behaviour of electrons ; but this does not prevent us from laying down a rule according to which the " reality " of what is said to be perceived is made to depend upon the conditions in which the perception occurs.[1] Thus, what is being asserted by those who speak of the table as being *really* a group of electrons is simply the hypothetical proposition that, in the conditions which they choose to regard as definitive of " reality ", the sort of sense-data that would be experienced would be those that are taken as verifying the relevant statements about electrons ; and this is not incompatible with the more normal view that the common-sense objects which people ordinarily think that they perceive are real ; for in this case it is the conditions which accompany such perceptions that are taken to be definitive of " reality " ; and there is no contradiction involved in the statement that, given different conditions, one will have different sorts of experiences. There appears to be a contradiction here, only because it is not seen that in such a context as this the word " reality " is apt to be ambiguous.[1]

The upshot, then, of this discussion of the causal theory of perception is that if a sense-datum has any

---

[1] This should be read in connexion with section 24 of this book, where I give an account of the principles by which I believe that our use of the word " reality " is governed.

cause at all it is to be sought among other sense-data. To the question, What are the causes of sense-data in general? there can indeed be no significant answer. For it does not make sense to postulate a cause of phenomena as a whole. But it is always permissible to attempt to correlate any given sense-datum, or " range " of sense-data, with another. It may, however, be objected that the word " cause " ought not to be applied at all to sense-data, both on account of its metaphysical associations, and because it is in any case a word that properly belongs to the terminology of material things ; and with this suggestion I am inclined to agree. But this does not affect my point that if a question as to the cause of a sense-datum is to be admitted at all, it must be understood as a question about the possibility of correlating the sense-datum with other sense-data, in such a way as to make its occurrence inferrible by the use of extrapolable laws.

The view that sense-data are causally dependent upon one another has been considered and rejected by some philosophers ; but the grounds on which they have rejected it have involved misapplications, or misunderstandings, of the notion of " causality ". Thus Berkeley, who used the word " idea " to stand for what was immediately perceived, declared that it was " impossible for an idea to do anything, or, strictly speaking, to be the cause of anything ", since " a little attention will discover to us that the very being of an idea implies passiveness and inertness in it ". And, in any case, " there is nothing in [ideas] but what is perceived ". " But whoever shall attend to his ideas, whether of sense or reflection, will not perceive in them any power or activity ; there is therefore no such thing contained in them." In other words, " all our ideas, sensations, or the things which we perceive, by whatsoever names they may be distinguished, are visibly inactive . . . so that *one idea* or object of thought *cannot produce,* or make *any alteration in another* ".[1] Now it is quite true that what Berkeley meant by " power or activity " is not anywhere to be detected in the objects that we perceive ; but the inference I draw from this is not that such objects cannot have causal properties, but rather that the term " cause " must, in this context, be divorced from the animistic notions of power and activity if it is to have any significant application. And indeed, in the sense in which I am interpreting " causality ", Berkeley himself agreed that " ideas " could cause one another ; for he regarded the " laws of nature " as *de facto* correlations of " ideas ".[2] Where he differed was in retaining, in addition to this concept of natural law, an animistic concept of causality, and in making the assumption that every idea must have a cause in this animistic sense. But this is an assumption for which there is not the least empirical evidence ; and it led, in Berkeley's case, to the senseless conclusion that only a God could be the cause of the great majority of our " ideas ".

[1] *The Principles of Human Knowledge*, ch. xxv.
[2] Cf. *Ibid.*, chs. xxx to xxxiii.

A final objection which it will be well to consider is one that has been most clearly stated by Professor Price. He argues that a " family of sense-data ", which he regards as an essential constituent of any material thing, cannot be the subject of the causal characteristics which are rightly attributed to the thing, on the ground that " the causal characteristics are actually being manifested in many parts of a region all at once, at a time when the family is actually being manifested only in one small part of it ; so that in most or perhaps all of the required places, the alleged subject of the characteristics just is not there to be the subject of them ".[1] For " how ", he asks, " can actual and manifest characteristics be said to characterize something at a time when the alleged *characterizandum* is but a system of potentialities ? "[2] Accordingly, he concludes that the family of sense-data must be coincident with what he calls a " physical occupant ", the sole function of which, so far as our knowledge is supposed to go, is to be the inferred subject of causal characteristics ; and it is the union of the family of sense-data and the physical occupant that, according to Price, makes up the complete object which we ordinarily describe as a material thing.

The way to answer this objection is to make clear once again what it is that we mean when we say of a material thing that it has this or that causal characteristic. Let us take Professor Price's own example of a stone wall which is said to be impenetrable. How, then, is such a statement verified ? Price him-

---

[1] *Perception*, p. 289. [2] *Ibid.* p. 291.

self gives the answer wholly in terms of sense-data. It is noticed that when a " foreign family " comes into contact with the family, or " the visuotactual nuclear solid " of the family, which goes to constitute the stone wall, the foreign family does not fuse with it, or prolong itself beyond it ; [1] " it begins to prolong itself in quite a new manner and usually in the opposite direction ". This, then, is what one observes when one observes something, say a tennis ball, failing to penetrate a stone wall. But it is believed that the stone wall continues to have the causal characteristic of impenetrability even when no one is observing any phenomena of the kind described. What then is involved in this ? No more, surely, than that if anyone were to observe any " foreign family " prolonging itself up to the family that con- stituted the stone wall, he would observe that it pro- longed itself subsequently in a different direction. In other words, the existence of the causal charac- teristic is, in such cases, a matter of the truth of a hypothetical proposition about sense-data ; and it is not in the least necessary for the validity of this hypothetical proposition, though it may be necessary for its actual verification, that the protasis should be realized. And we get the same result if we analyse any other of Price's examples, say that of the mag- netized bar which is concealed in a man's pocket.[2]

---

[1] *Perception*, p. 278. The use of statements referring to the behaviour of " families " of sense-data is, of course, to be under- stood only as a convenient way of referring to the relationships of individual sense-data, which are constituents of the " families " in question.   [2] *Ibid*. p. 290.

Here, a compass needle is seen to be deflected. No actual sense-data of the magnet family exist; but the magnetic field is actual. Does not this prove that the family cannot itself have the causal characteristic of being magnetic? I am sure that it does not. For all that one has to say in such a case is that the sense-data, in virtue of which it is asserted that a compass needle is being deflected, would not be occurring in the given conditions unless sense-data belonging to the magnet family were obtainable. That is to say, one is expressing a complex proposition of the form " p, and, if p, then, if q, then r ". And for the validity of this proposition it is necessary, not that either q, which here refers to the existence of the conditions in which sense-data of the magnet are expected to occur, or r, which here refers to the actual occurrence of such sense-data, should be true, but only that it should be true that if q, then r. And any other example that might be given could be dealt with in the same way.

I conclude, then, that the argument by means of which Professor Price attempts to show that families of sense-data cannot have causal characteristics is invalid; and, consequently, I cannot accept his reason for assuming the reality of " physical occupants ". Nor does there appear to be any other reason for believing in the existence of these mysterious entities, about whose " intrinsic qualities " their sponsor himself maintains that " we have no knowledge at all, and no prospect of getting any ".[1]

[1] *Perception*, p. 321.

V

THE CONSTITUTION OF MATERIAL THINGS

22. Concerning Phenomenalism

The problem of specifying the relationship of material things to sense-data, to which the causal theory of perception has been shown to provide so unsatisfactory an answer, is apt to be obscured by being represented as a problem about the inter-relationship of two different classes of objects. There is, indeed, a sense in which it is correct to say that both sense-data and material things exist, inasmuch as sentences that are used to describe sense-data and sentences that are used to describe material things both very frequently express true propositions. But it would not be correct to infer from this that there really were both material things and sense-data, in the sense in which it can truly be said that there really are chairs as well as tables, or that there are tastes as well as sounds. For whereas, in these cases, the existential propositions refer to different empirical " facts ", this does not hold good in the case of sense-data and material things. All the same, the term " material thing " is not synonymous with any term or set of terms that stand for species of sense-data. It is indeed logically necessary that any situation that in any degree establishes the existence of a material thing should also establish the existence of a sense-datum ; for we have constructed the sense-datum language in such a way that whenever it is true that a material thing is perceived, it must also be true that a sense-datum is sensed ; and this applies also to the cases where the existence of the material thing is inferred from observations of its " physical effects ". But it is not wholly a matter of convention that a situation which establishes the existence of a sense-datum should also be evidence in some degree for the existence of a material thing. For this depends, as I shall show, upon certain special features of our sensory experience, which it might conceivably not have possessed. Moreover, while a situation which directly establishes the existence of a sense-datum does so conclusively, no such situations can conclusively establish the existence of a material thing. The degree to which the existence of the material thing is established will depend upon the character of the sense-data in question, and especially upon the nature of the contexts in which they occur ; but whatever the strength of this evidence may be, it will always be logically compatible with the hypothesis that this material thing is not in all respects what it appears to be, or even that it does not exist at all. Additional evidence may weaken this hypothesis to an extent that makes it very foolish still to entertain it ; but it may also substantiate it, as the fact that there are illusions shows. At the same time, it is to be remarked that this additional evidence, whether favourable or not, will always consist in the occurrence of further sense-data. Indeed there is nothing else in which one can legitimately suppose it to consist, once one has accepted the rule that the word " sense-datum " is to be used to stand for whatever is, in fact, observed. And since it is impossible, by any valid process of inference, to make a transition from what is observed to anything that is conceived as being, in principle, unobservable, all that the evidence in question will be evidence for or against is the possible occurrence of further sense-data still. And from this it seems to follow that, even though the term " material thing " is not synonymous with any set of terms that stand for species of sense-data, any proposition that refers to a material thing must somehow be expressible in terms of sense-data, if it is to be empirically significant.

A common way of expressing this conclusion is to say that material things are nothing but collections of actual and possible sense-data. But this is a misleading formula and one that provokes objections which a more accurate way of speaking might avoid. Thus, it is sometimes argued, by those who reject this " phenomenalistic " analysis of the nature of material things, that to conceive of such things as houses or trees or stones as mere collections of actual and possible sense-data is to ignore their " unity " and " substantiality ", and that, in any case, it is hard to see how anything can be composed of so shadowy a being as a possible sense-datum. But these objections are founded upon the mistaken assumption that a material thing is supposed to consist of sense-data, as a patchwork quilt consists of different coloured pieces of silk. To remove this misconception, it must be made clear that what the statement that material things consist of sense-data must be understood to designate is not a factual but a linguistic relationship. What is being claimed is simply that the propositions which are ordinarily expressed by sentences which refer to material things could also be expressed by sentences which referred exclusively to sense-data; and the inclusion of possible as well as actual sense-data among the elements of the material things must be taken only to imply a recognition that some of these statements about sense-data will have to be hypothetical. As for the belief in the " unity " and " substantiality " of material things, I shall show that it may be correctly represented as involving no more than the attribution to visual and tactual sense-data of certain relations which do, in fact, obtain in our experience. And I shall show that it is only the contingent fact that there are these relations between sense-data that makes it profitable to describe the course of our experience in terms of the existence and behaviour of material things.

It may seem that an attempt to carry out this plan of " reducing " material things to sense-data would be at variance with my previous attempt to draw a sharp distinction between them. But the purpose of making this distinction was simply to increase the utility and clarity of the sense-datum language by ensuring that its sentences should not be of the same logical form as those that refer to material things. And here it may be explained that two sentences may be said to have the same logical form if they can be correlated in such a way that to each expression that occurs in either one of them there corresponds in the other an expression of the same logical type ; and that two expressions may be said to be of the same logical type if any sentence that significantly contains either one of them remains significant when the other is put in its place. It follows that if sentences referring to sense-data are of a different logical form from sentences referring to material things, it must not be assumed that precisely the same things can be said about them. To say, for example, that this was being written with a " pennish " group of sense-data, instead of saying that it was being written with a pen, would be neither true nor false but nonsensical. But this does not rule out the possibility that a proposition which is expressed by a sentence referring to a material thing can equally well be expressed by an entirely different set of sentences, which refer to sense-data ; and this is what those who assert that material things are " logical constructions " out of sense-data must be understood to claim. Their view is sometimes put in the form of an assertion that " to say anything about a material thing is to say something, but not the same thing about classes of sense-data " ;[1] but if this is taken to imply that any

[1] *Vide* A. E. Duncan-Jones, " Does Philosophy Analyse Common Sense ? " *Aristotelian Society Supplementary Proceedings*, 1937, pp. 140-41.

significant statement about a material thing can actually be translated, without alteration of meaning, into a definite set of statements about sense-data, it is not strictly accurate, for a reason I shall presently give.

An objection which is often brought against phenomenalists is that they begin with a false conception of the nature of " perceptual situations ". Thus, it is held by some philosophers that what is directly observed is usually not a sense-datum at all, but a material thing ; so that the view that material things must be reducible to sense-data, on the ground that these alone are observable, is fundamentally erroneous. But this, as I have shown,[1] is not the expression of a disagreement about any matter of fact, but only of a preference for a different form of language. It is indeed legitimate to use the phrase " direct observation " in such a way that things like houses and trees and stones can properly be said to be directly observable ; and this usage can perfectly well be made to cover the case of delusive as well as veridical perceptions, provided that it is allowed that what is " directly observed " may not in fact exist, and that it may not really have the properties that it appears to have. But I have shown that it is also legitimate to use the phrase " direct observation " in such a way that it is only what is designated by the term " sense-datum ", or some equivalent term, that can be said to be directly observable ; and that it is this usage that, for my present purpose, is to be preferred. And one reason why it is to be preferred is to be found in the

[1] In Part I.

fact, which I have already mentioned, that whereas the proposition that a sense-datum is veridically sensed does not entail that any material thing is veridically perceived, the proposition that a material thing is veridically perceived can always be represented as entailing that some sense-datum or other is veridically sensed. Indeed, it is inconceivable that any sense-datum should not be sensed veridically, since it has been made self-contradictory to say of an experienced sense-datum that it does not exist or that it does not really have the properties that it appears to have. And because there is this logical relationship between " perceiving a material thing " and " sensing a sense-datum ", it follows that, while a reference to a material thing will not elucidate the meaning of a sentence which is used to describe a sense-datum, except in so far as the poverty of our language may make it convenient to identify this sense-datum as one of a type that is ordinarily associated with a special sort of material thing, a reference to sense-data will provide a general elucidation of the meaning of statements about material things by showing what is the kind of evidence by which they may be verified. And this may be regarded as the purpose of the phenomenalist analysis.

Besides the philosophers who maintain that material things are themselves " directly observed ", there are others who object to phenomenalism on the ground that even if the occurrence of illusions shows that what is directly observed is not a material thing, it is still not just a sense-datum. Thus Professor Stout, for one, has argued that " the evidence of sense-perception flatly contradicts phenomenalism ", on the ground that to regard what is immediately experienced as being just a sensible appearance is to ignore an essential factor which he calls " perceptual seeming ".[1] According to him, it is because of " perceptual seeming " that one is able to " perceive one thing as behind another, although it is so hidden that there is no sensible appearance of it ", or that one can " perceive things as having insides, when they are not transparent ".[2] But while this line of argument may have some force against those who employ a physiological criterion for determining the character of sense-data, it does not affect us at all, inasmuch as our use of the word sense-datum is not bound up with any special empirical theory about the nature of what is given. If one accepts the view of certain psychologists that there are experiences that may properly be described as experiences of " seeing the inside of a solid object " or " seeing an object when it is screened by another ", then the inference one must draw is not that what is observed on such occasions is " more than a mere sense-datum ", but that the character of people's visual sense-fields is empirically different from what a misplaced attention to the laws of physiology might lead one to suppose. It is true that the terms in which the psychologists describe such experiences are not

---

[1] " Phenomenalism ", *Proceedings of the Aristotelian Society*, 1938–9, pp. 1-18.　　　　[2] *Loc. cit.* pp. 10-11.

purely sensory ; but the reason for this is that it is only by referring to material things that they can actually expect to make their meaning understood. We must not, therefore, be misled into supposing that what they are intending to describe is anything more than a sensory phenomenon. The statement that someone is having the experience of " seeing the inside of a solid object " must not, in this context, be taken to exclude the possibility that no such physical object is actually there.

It may, however, be admitted that not only in cases of this sort, but in the vast majority of cases in which one senses a visual or tactual sense-datum, one tends to take it for granted that there is a physical object " there " ; and it may be that this is what Professor Stout is referring to when he talks of " perceptual seeming ". But this is a fact that I do not think any phenomenalist would wish to deny. The view that material things are, in the sense I have just explained, logical constructions out of sense-data does not imply that " perceiving a material thing " need involve any conscious process of infer-ence from the occurrence of one sense-datum to the possible occurrence of another. The phenomenalist is perfectly free to admit that the sensing of a visual or tactual sense-datum is, in most cases, accompanied by an unreflecting assumption of the existence of some material thing. But the question in which he is interested is, What exactly is it that is here un-reflectingly assumed ? And his answer, which certainly cannot be refuted by any such appeal to psychology as Professor Stout relies on, is that it is the possibility of obtaining further sense-data.

It would seem that the best way to justify the claim that " to say anything about a material thing is always to say something, though not the same thing, about certain sense-data ", would be to provide a number of specimen translations. But this is what no one has ever yet been able to do. It may be suggested that the reason why it has never been done is that no one has yet devised a sufficiently elaborate vocabulary. With our current resources of language we are able to classify visual sense-data only in a very general way, tactual data even less specifically, and kinaesthetic data hardly at all : and the result is that when we wish to distinguish the sense-data that belong to one sort of material thing from those that belong to another we are unable to achieve it except by referring to the material things in question. But suppose that someone took the trouble to name all the different varieties of sensible characteristics with which he was acquainted. Even so, he would still not be able to translate any statement about a material thing into a finite set of statements about sense-data. It is not inconceivable that someone should construct and make use of such a sensory language, though in practice he would find it very difficult to make himself understood ; but what he succeeded in expressing by these means would never be precisely equivalent even to the singular statements that we make about material things. For when statements are equivalent to one another, they can always be represented as standing in a relationship of mutual entailment. And, in the case I am now considering, this condition cannot be fulfilled.

I have indeed already admitted that no finite set of singular statements about sense-data can ever formally entail a statement about a material thing, inasmuch as I have recognized that statements about material things are not conclusively verifiable. For when we try to reproduce the content of a statement about a material thing by specifying the empirical situations that would furnish us with direct tests of its validity, we find that the number of these possible tests is infinite. Admittedly, when someone makes a statement of this kind he does not actually envisage an infinite series of possible verifications. He may very well be satisfied, in familiar circumstances, with the single sense-experience on which his statement is based ; and if he does think it necessary to test it further, the subsequent occurrence, in the appropriate conditions, of only a limited number of " favourable " sense-data will be sufficient, in the absence of contrary evidence, to convince him that it is true. And this is an entirely reasonable procedure, as I have shown.[1] But the fact remains that however many favourable tests he may make he can never reach a stage at which it ceases to be conceivable that further sense-experience will reverse the verdict of the previous evidence. He will never be in a position to demonstrate that he will not subsequently

[1] Part I, section 4.

have experiences that will entitle him to conclude that his original statement was false after all. And this implies that the content of a statement about a material thing cannot be exhaustively specified by any finite number of references to sense-data. This difficulty could indeed be met by introducing into the sense-datum language a suitable set of expressions which would be understood to refer to infinite series of sense-data. But I am afraid that most philosophers would not admit that this gave them the sort of translation that they wanted. For all that would seem to be achieved by the introduction of these new expressions would be a mere renaming of material things.

But not only is the occurrence of any one particular, finite series of sense-data never formally sufficient to establish the truth of a statement about a material thing ; it is never even necessary. There is, indeed, a sense in which it can be said that every statement about a material thing entails some set of statements or other about sense-data, inasmuch as it is only by the occurrence of some sense-datum that any statement about a material thing is ever in any degree verified. But there is no set of statements about the occurrence of particular sense-data of which it can truly be said that precisely this is entailed by a given statement about a material thing. And the reason for this is that what is required to verify a statement about a material thing is never just the occurrence of a sense-datum of an absolutely specific kind, but only the occurrence of one or other of the sense-data that fall within a fairly indefinite range. In other words, not only can we go on testing a statement about a material thing as long as we like without being able to arrive at a formal demonstration of its truth ; but for any test that we actually do carry out there are always an in-definite number of other tests, differing to some extent either in respect of their conditions or their results, which would have done just as well. And this means that if we try to describe what at any given moment would afford us direct evidence for the truth of a statement about a material thing by putting forward a disjunction of statements about sense-data, we shall find once again that this dis-junction will have to be infinite.[1]

But if one infers from this that sentences referring to material things cannot be translated, without alteration of meaning, into sentences referring to sense-data, one must not then conclude that to speak about a material thing is to speak about some-thing altogether different from sense-data, or that it is to speak about sense-data but about something else besides. For that would be a mistake analogous to that of supposing that because sentences referring indefinitely to what is red cannot be translated into a finite number of sentences referring to particular red things, therefore " redness " is the name of an object with a distinct existence of its own, or that be-cause sentences referring to " someone " cannot be

---

[1] Cf. John Wisdom, " Metaphysics and Verification ", *Mind*, October 1938, pp 478-81.

translated into a finite disjunction of sentences referring to particular persons, therefore " someone " is
the name of a peculiar being, a " subsistent entity "
perhaps, who is distinct from any person that one can
actually meet. If we cannot produce the required
translations of sentences referring to material things
into sentences referring to sense-data, the reason is
not that it is untrue that " to say anything about a
material thing is always to say something about
sense-data ", but only that one's references to
material things are vague in their application to
phenomena and that the series of sense-data that
they may be understood to specify are composed of
infinite sets of terms.

This does not mean, however, that nothing can
be done in the way of " analysing material things in
terms of sense-data ". It would not, indeed, be
profitable to seek in any such analysis a means of
distinguishing one material thing from another. It
is not by a verbal analysis in terms of sense-data
that one can hope to make clear what is meant, for
example, by " a pen " as opposed to " a pencil ", or
by " a steamship " as opposed to " a canoe ". One
can give a verbal, as well as an ostensive, indication
of the meaning of such words ; but it will not
exclude the use of other expressions that belong to a
physical rather than to a purely sensory terminology.
At the same time, there are certain general features
about the way in which any expression referring to a
material thing applies to phenomena that one can
profitably undertake to analyse. That is to say, one

may be able to explain what are the relations between sense-data that make it possible for us successfully to employ the physical terminology that we do. If I may now use the metaphor of construction without being misunderstood, I can describe the task I am about to undertake as that of showing what are the general principles on which, from our resources of sense-data, we " construct " the world of material things.

23. ELEMENTARY CONSTRUCTION OF THE MATERIAL WORLD

The main problem which lies before me is that of answering Hume's question why it is that " we attribute a *continued* existence to objects even when they are not present to the senses ; and why we suppose them to have an existence *distinct* from perception ".[1] Hume himself interpreted this as a question about the sources of an illusion. He saw that the " philosophical " assumption that besides one's perceptions, which alone were directly given, there existed an independent set of objects, of which one's perceptions were copies or effects, was an entirely unwarrantable re-duplication of the perceptual world ; and since he held that it was self-contradictory to suppose that any "perception" itself could exist unsensed, he came to the conclusion that the belief in the continued and distinct existence of objects was a fallacious product of the imagination.

[1] Vide *A Treatise of Human Nature*, Book I, Part IV, section ii.

What he did not see was that the relations of
" constancy " and " coherence " between sense-data
in which he discovered the source of this supposed
illusion could themselves be taken as definitive of the
continued and distinct existence of objects. But
what precisely are these relations of constancy and
coherence? And how do they make it possible for us
to describe our sense-data, which are conceived to be
transitory and private, by the use of expressions which
ostensibly refer to substances which are supposed
to endure unperceived, to be endowed with causal
properties, to be accessible to different senses and
to different observers, and to stand to one another
in the system of relations that constitutes their being
in " physical space "? With the question of the
publicity of these material things, and the way in
which it is compatible with the privacy of sense-data,
I have already dealt. And I have given an indication
of what we mean by attributing causal properties to
them, and of the grounds on which we conceive them
as able to exist unperceived. But a more detailed
explanation is required of the nature of our " construction " of physical space, and of what Hume
called " the principle of identity ", in virtue of which
we derive from successive sense-data the conception
of a single, persistent material thing.

An outline of what I take to be the correct view
of these matters was given by John Stuart Mill when
he spoke of physical bodies as " permanent possibilities of sensation ". He explains very well how
it is that " a group of sensations ", which are mainly

" conceived in the form of present possibilities ",
" presents itself to the mind as permanent, in contrast not solely with the temporariness of one's
bodily presence, but also with the temporary character of each of the sensations composing the group ;
in other words as a kind of permanent substratum,
under a set of passing experiences or manifestations ";
and how it is that " we learn to think of nature as
made up solely of these groups of possibilities, and
the active force in nature as manifested in the modifi-
cation of some of these by others " ; while " the
sensations, though the original foundation of the
whole, come to be looked upon as a sort of accident
depending on us, and the possibilities as much more
real than the actual sensations, nay, as the very
realities of which these are only the representations,
appearances, or effects ".[1] But some account is
required of the manner in which these groups are
formed ; and we cannot here be satisfied, as Mill
apparently was, with a vague reference to " the laws
of the association of ideas ". For sense-data may be
associated, both in fact and in thought, in many ways
that are not relevant to the issue ; nor is it every
kind of well-founded hypothetical proposition about
sense-data that enters into the conception of the
continued existence of material things. Moreover,
Mill was at fault in supposing that, in the case of the
" primary qualities " of material things, visual sensations were merely " *symbols* of tactual and muscular

---

[1] *An Examination of Sir William Hamilton's Philosophy*, pp.
194-5.

I

ones ".[1] This mistake, which was made also by Berkeley in his *Theory of Vision*, may perhaps be due to a failure to distinguish properly between physical and sensible space. It is true that the conception of the physical situation of a material thing involves, as we shall see, a reference to the possible movements of an observer, and so to kinaesthetic data, though even here it would be inaccurate to speak of the visual data as symbols of the kinaesthetic; but this does not mean that any reference to kinaesthetic data is required for the ascription of spatial properties to visual sense-data themselves. The extension and figure of a visual sense-datum are sensibly " given " no less than its colour ; and so are its spatial relations to other sense-data within the same visual field, including its " distance " from sense-data which belong to the body of the observer. For the visual sense-field is sensibly three-dimensional. And while it is true that the data out of which the material world is " constructed " are not drawn from the sense of sight alone, it is, for those who can obtain them, the visual and not the tactual data that are of primary importance. In either case, what interests us in the present context is not so much the qualities of the individual sense-data as the relations which obtain between them, and especially the relations which obtain between sense-data which are constituents of different sense-fields. Now, whatever may be the difference in content between visual and tactual experiences, it does not

[1] *Op. cit.* p. 237.

prevent their having a close similarity of structure ; and it is because of this similarity of structure that one finds it natural to regard a visual and a tactual " construct " as one and the same material thing. Accordingly, if one is able to give an account of the principles which are involved in the construction of the physical world out of either visual or tactual sense-data, the case of the other sense will present no special problem ; and since ordinary language is chiefly adapted to the description of visual phenomena I shall confine myself to them.

At the present moment I am aware of a visual sense-field the contents of which I may describe by saying that I am perceiving, among other things, a table covered with papers, and beyond the table a chair, and beyond the chair a section of a book-case fastened to a wall. If I now turn aside to look out of the window on my right, these particular sense-data cease to exist, and in their place I obtain a new set of visual sense-data which I may describe by saying that I am perceiving a garden fringed with trees, and beyond the trees the roof of a cottage, and in the distance a thickly wooded hill. And if I execute a further movement, I shall find that these sense-data too will cease to exist, and that others will take their place. But suppose that at some stage in a process of this kind I reverse the direction of my movements. In that case I shall find that this fragment of my sense-history repeats itself, but in a reverse order. I do not mean by this

that I shall sense numerically the same sense-data
as I sensed before; for that is excluded by the
conventions of the sense-datum language. But there
will be a general resemblance between these two
sections of my experience; so that I shall find not
merely that individual sense-data are closely similar
to ones that I sensed before, but that they occur in
similar contexts. In the end I shall have a sense-field
whose similarity to the first will make it proper for me
to describe it by saying that I am again perceiving a
table, a chair and a book-case, related as before; but
whereas, in the previous case, the sense-field which
I described in this way preceded the sense-field
which I described by referring to a garden fringed
with trees, in the case of their counterparts this order
will be reversed. And in whatever direction I may
move away from my original point of view, I find
that I can always obtain a " reversible " series of
this sort, beginning and ending with a sense-field of
a kind that I habitually describe in the same way as
that with which my account of this experiment
began. And I find also that I am able to obtain any
number of " reversible " series in which a sense-
field of this kind occurs, not as an end but as a
middle term.[1] In some cases, indeed, the " reproduction " of a term in such a series is not perfect;
for I may have experiences that would ordinarily be
described by saying that some particular thing had

[1] For the importance of this possibility of " reversion " cf. Eino
Kaila, " Über das System der Wirklichkeitsbegriffe ", *Acta Philo-
sophica Fennica*, Fasc. 2, 1936, pp. 29-33. I am much indebted
to him.

altered its position, or undergone a change of quality, or even that it had ceased to exist altogether. But all such changes take place within a relatively stable environment. The sense-data by which they are manifested do not have counterparts in the relevant strand of my previous experience ; but they occur in contexts that do have the requisite counterparts ; and it is only because this is so that I am able to classify them in the way that I do.[1]

Ignoring, for the moment, the problem of illusory experiences, with which I shall deal later on, I shall now try to generalize this example in such a way as to indicate the nature of the " laws of sensory association " which give rise to our conception of the material world. I suggest that our grouping of sense-data to form particular material things is governed by four main conditions, which I shall now set forth.

The first set of relations which obtain between the different sense-data that enter into the constitution of the same material thing are relations of resemblance. For reasons which I have already given,[2] I am not able to say what these relations are in any particular case except by referring to the kind of material thing in question ; but there is no foundation here for a charge of circularity, since the point is not that I must already have a conception of the material thing in order to be able to discover these relations, but only that I have no other means

---

[1] Cf. Kaila, *op. cit.* pp. 59-60.   [2] P. 238 ff.

of describing them. It may, however, be objected that one's field of vision does not always comprise even the appearance of the whole of a single surface of a material thing, let alone an appearance of all the surfaces of what is presumed to be " a three-dimensional solid " ; and that there is often very little resemblance between the appearances of one part of the thing and those of another. But while the sense-data that are supposed to belong to different parts of the same material thing may not resemble one another directly to any great extent, they do stand in what may be called a relation of indirect resemblance, in virtue of the fact that they can be linked by a series of sense-data which do directly resemble one another. For it is possible, by making suitable movements, to sense a series of sense-fields which I can find no better way to describe than by saying that they reveal partially overlapping aspects of the thing in question ; and while there may be considerable differences in content between sense-fields which are remote from one another in the series, the differences between its adjacent members will be very small. And by this means one can provide oneself also with a set of sense-data which can be fitted together in the imagination, like the pieces of a jigsaw puzzle, in such a way as to yield a complete picture of the object, which may never as a whole be given to sense. And there will be what I may call a relation of " global resemblance " between any two series of sense-data that make up the complete views of the object that are obtainable at different periods of time.[1]

That this relation admits of various degrees is shown by the fact that we allow it to be possible for the material thing to change without thereby losing its identity. But how far such changes may go before it becomes correct to say that the original thing has ceased to exist, and has been replaced by another, is a question that is not subject to any exact set of rules. In any case, one's attribution of numerical identity to a material thing depends not only upon the degree of resemblance that is displayed by the sense-data that one takes to belong to it, but also upon one's finding that they occur in similar contexts. And this brings me to the second of my four conditions ; which is, that for similar sense-data to be elements of numerically the same material thing, they must, generally speaking, occur in a similar sensible environment. I say " generally speaking " to allow for the fact that the thing may sometimes move ; but here again there is a relation of indirect resemblance between the sensible environments. For one's judgement that an object which has moved is numerically the same as that which previously existed in another place involves

---

[1] A very full and good account of this, the first of my four conditions, is given by Professor Price in his chapter in " The Relation of Sense-data to One Another ", *Perception*, ch. viii. But he seems occasionally to confuse sensible and physical space, as when he speaks of an unsensed sense-datum as being " literally beyond " one that is being sensed (cf. pp. 240-43), and he seems to have overlooked the importance of my other conditions, particularly the second and third.

an assumption that one could have "traced its
path" through a series of partially overlapping sense-
fields, of which any two adjacent members would
have been directly resemblant. And this assumption
is grounded on the fact that in many cases this
"possibility of sensation" is actually realized. I
include also under this heading of the constancy of
the sensible environment the criterion of a thing's
self-identity which consists in its retaining the same
causal properties. For this amounts only to a
temporal extension of the context for which the
similarity is required.

Now were this condition of the recurrence of
similar contexts not, in fact, fulfilled in our experience, as it conceivably might not have been, we
should not have any grounds for identifying particular material things in the way that we do. Given
the necessary resemblances between sense-data, we
should be able to find a use for words that stand for
different species of material things, but unless such
sense-data occurred, as they actually do, in a
relatively constant sensible environment, we should
not, with our current rules of self-identity, be able
to distinguish particular instances of these species
and assign to each of them an individual history.
Moreover, our conception of these things as enduring
through time, and occupying definite positions in
"physical space" involves the fulfilment of a further
condition ; which is that the relevant sorts of sense-
data should be systematically reproducible in the
way that was indicated by my illustration. To

provide a more imaginative illustration, which may
help to show how this condition operates, I shall
now have recourse to a different class of sense-data,
the phenomena of sounds. For Caliban " the isle
was full of noises " which he was not able to identify
as the " effects " of any physical sources ; and one
may assume that the noises came to him in patterns
and that these patterns were fairly constantly repeated, in the ordinary sense in which a song may be
said to be repeated when the singer gives an encore.
But suppose that the sounds exhibited a more
extensive uniformity, the sort of uniformity that is
actually displayed by visual and tactual sense-data
in our everyday experience. Imagine a Caliban,
devoid of the senses of sight and touch, but endowed
with highly differentiated kinaesthetic sensations, in
terms of which he was able to distinguish different
directions of movement ; and suppose that he found
that with every kinaesthetic series, which constituted
his movement " from one place to another ", there
was associated a special type of auditory series which
was reinstated in a reverse order when the direction
of his movements was reversed. In that case it
would be natural for him to construct a " physical
space " of sounds and to conceive of them as persist-
ing in it unheard, just as out of visual and tactual
sense-data we construct a physical space which we
people with persistent sensibilia in the form of
material things. He would say that a sound which
he heard on different occasions was the same, not
merely in the qualitative sense of sameness in which

a musician who gives an encore may be said to play the same tune as before, but in a numerical sense analogous to that in which I may say of the pen with which I am now writing that it is the same as that with which I was writing yesterday. If he were addicted to philosophizing he might even come to distinguish between auditory sense-data, or " ideas of sound ", which he would regard as momentary objects, incapable of existing unperceived, and auditory things, to which he would attribute " a continued and distinct existence " ; and then he might perplex himself with the question how the existence of these things could be inferred from the occurrence of the sense-data, which alone were directly given. And this would not be a more artificial problem than that which the peculiar structure of our visual and tactual experience has actually led philosophers to raise about " our knowledge of the external world ".[1]

For us there is no problem of the self-identity of particular sounds since we do not subject them, any more than we subject tastes or smells, to the category

[1] Kaila (*op. cit.* pp. 35-9) makes use of a similar example. But he seems to suggest that a person who constructed a world of auditory things, in such conditions as I have described, would be subject to an illusion, and says that " we can laugh at his naïvety, because we possess a more comprehensive sense, our sense of sight, which affords us a *simultaneous* conspectus of our blind man's world, while he can apprehend it only in the form of an acoustical kinaesthetic *succession* ". I should say, however, that the construction of auditory things was a correct and reasonable way for my Caliban to describe his experience, and that the possession of a mere comprehensive sense of *sight* would not necessarily make any difference in this context, except in so far as it introduced a problem about the relationship of visual and auditory " space ".

of substance. We find it more convenient to regard
the data of these senses as adjectival to the visuo-
tactual constructs to which, on the basis of observed
correlations, they are referred as qualities or effects.
It is true that we do allow ourselves to speak of a
sound as existing unsensed, in cases where we
believe that if someone were to be in the relevant
position he would be hearing it ; but we do not
admit the possibility of hearing numerically the same
sound on different occasions, in the sense in which
we suppose that we are able to perceive numerically
the same material thing. If we speak of " hearing
the same sound " it is only in an analogous sense to
that in which we speak of " seeing the same colour "
or " feeling the same pain ". We do not identify
the sound as a particular with any one that has been
heard before or could be heard after. What we
mean by saying that it is the same sound as one that
is heard on some other occasion is that it exhibits
the same character, or, in other words, that it is a
different particular instance of the same " universal ".
The criterion in this case is simply that of qualitative
resemblance. And the reason why we do not find
it useful to substantialize sounds, in the way that we
substantialize groups of visual and tactual sense-
data, is that the condition of " systematic reproduction " is not fulfilled in the requisite way by auditory
sense-fields. But it is easy to conceive that it might
have been fulfilled by them, just as it is easy to
conceive that it might not have been fulfilled in the
case of our visual and tactual experiences. It is a

contingent fact that any domain of sense-experience possesses the structure that makes it convenient for us to apply to it the language that we do.

At this point it may be objected that the fact that one does not make substances out of auditory sense-data proves that I was wrong to accept Mill's doctrine of " permanent possibilities of sensation ". For if this, it may be said, is to be taken as the criterion of " continued and distinct existence ", then the world must be literally much more " full of noises " than it is supposed to be. For example, I am not now hearing the sound of my front-door bell ; nor do I believe that it is being heard by anyone else ; but I have good reason to believe the hypothetical proposition that if at any time I were to have such experiences as are associated with ringing this bell, I should then have the sensation of hearing it ; and this would apply to a multitude of other sounds that are not actually believed to exist. And the same objection can be raised with regard to visual sense-data. For example, it is a " conditional certainty ", in Mill's sense,[1] that if at any time I were to have such experiences as would constitute my heating the water in my kettle to boiling point, I should then obtain some visual sense-data which I might describe by saying that I was seeing steam issuing from it ; yet while I believe that the kettle exists unperceived, I do not believe this to be true of the steam. But this difficulty is met by the

---

[1] Vide *An Examination of Sir William Hamilton's Philosophy* p. 193.

introduction of my fourth condition ; which is, that for a permanent possibility of sensation to be definitive of the continued and distinct existence of a material thing, its realization must be viewed as depending, apart from the fulfilment of the " standing conditions " which are required for the occurrence of any sense-data of the relevant sense,[1] only upon the movements of the observer. Thus I believe that the kettle now exists because I believe that if I were in the appropriate position, at which I could arrive by carrying out a given series of movements, I should be experiencing a visual or tactual sense-datum of it ; but I do not believe this to be true of the steam, and therefore I do not believe that it now exists. The reference to what I have called the " standing conditions ", such as the state of the light or of the nervous system of the observer, is not of importance in this context ; for they are present also in the case where a permanent possibility of sensation is not taken to be constitutive of a persistent material thing ; and they are not therefore relevant to the problem of distinguishing between this case and the other. Nor does the consideration of these standing conditions carry us outside the domain of actual and possible sense-data. For the belief in the necessity of these conditions may be founded on the observation, in particular cases, that unless sense-data that verify the presence of these conditions are obtainable, other sense-data of the relevant sense do not occur, or else upon the observation that the

[1] *Vide* p. 178.

others vary in accordance with them. And then these conclusions are legitimately generalized so as to cover even the occurrence of the sense-data that at any given moment are constitutive of the state of the conditions themselves.

As for the observer's awareness of his own movements, it is based upon kinaesthetic sensations, supplemented by the evidence of sight and touch ; and this evidence consists in the fact that members of the group of resemblant sense-data which are elements of the observer's body are found to succeed one another in a changing visual and tactual environment. It might be thought that a reference to the changes in the sensible environment would be sufficient, without our having to bring in any kinaesthetic sense-data, or even any visual or tactual sense-data of the observer's body. And this is, for example, the view of Professor Price, who maintains that " a purely visual being, *i.e.* one having no sense but sight, could know that he had a point of view and that he was changing it thus and thus ", and further that " a visual percipient without any body at all could have a point of view and change it just as we can ".[1] But to arrive at this conclusion he has to assume that his visual percipient is able to know that the sense-data which he successively experiences are constituents of different " standard solids ", which are situated at different places in physical space ; and I do not think that this assumption is justifiable. For I think that it is only by

---

[1] *Perception*, p. 255.

correlating such sense-data, in the manner I have described, with the series of his movements that he would be able to construct the physical system at all ; so that his original grounds for believing that he was altering his point of view could not consist solely in his observation of the changes in his environment. Once he had constructed the physical system, he would indeed be able to make use of it for his own orientation, and to conceive of its physical constituents as maintaining their relative spatial positions independently of any movements that he or any other observer might actually execute. But this does not mean that we can dispense with our reference to the observer's movements in giving an account of the principles that enter into this " construction " itself.

I hold, then, that the main features of the structure of our visual experience which give rise to our conception of material things are, first, the relations of resemblance between individual sense-data ; secondly, the comparative stability of the contexts in which these resemblant sense-data occur ; thirdly, the fact that the occurrence of such sense-data is systematically repeatable, in the way I have tried to indicate ; and fourthly, the dependence of this repetition upon the movements of the observer. These features are reproduced, albeit less clearly, in the structure of our tactual experience ; and it is, as I have said, this structural correspondence that makes it possible for us to combine our visual and tactual constructs to form particular material things.

Once one has accounted for the attribution of " continued and distinct existence " to material things, it is not very difficult to sketch out an analysis of our conception of physical space. The main problem here is to explain how the spatial relations that are " given " as obtaining between different constituents of single sense-fields can be used to define the relative positions of different material things, even when these are not capable of being simultaneously perceived. And for this I shall have recourse to a simple example. Consider the case of two material things A and M, which are conceived to be situated at places that are physically accessible from one another, but at such a distance that it is impossible to see them both at once. It follows that no sense-datum a of A will ever be observed to stand in a direct spatial relationship to any sense-datum m of M. But, by carrying out a suitable series of movements, it will be possible to obtain a series of " partially overlapping " sense-fields such that a is observed to stand in the spatial relation r to another sense-datum b, a sense-datum of the same kind as b is observed to stand in the relation r to another sense-datum c, a sense-datum of the same kind as c is observed to stand in the relation r to another sense-datum d, and, finally, to omit the intervening stages of the process, a sense-datum of the same kind as l is observed to stand in the relation r to m. Then, just as the groups of transient sense-data of which a and m are representatives are transformed, in accordance with the principles I have described, into the persistent material things A and M, so the relation r is transformed into the higher order relation R, which is supposed to obtain between material things even when no actual sense-data of them are being observed to be related by r, and even in cases where the possibility of linking the relevant sense-data consists, not in the power to observe a direct relation between them, but only in the power to establish an indirect relation such as obtained between a and m in my example. And thus one arrives at the conception of M as standing in the direction R from A, and also, since this process of spatial linking is reversible, at that of A as standing in the converse direction to R from M. The next step is to remove the restriction which I described by saying that M was physically accessible from A, by allowing that M may be said to stand in the direction R from A even when the establishment of the indirect relation between the relevant sense-data, though possible in principle, is, as the result of some hindrance to the movements of the observer, incapable of being realized in fact.

Now, it is characteristic of the sense-given spatial relations with which we are here concerned, first, that if a sense-datum x stands in any such relation r to another sense-datum y, then it is not the case that y also has r to x ; secondly, that if, within a single sense-field, x has r to y and y has r to another sense-datum z, then x has r to z ; and thirdly, that every sense-datum is either directly related by r to another constituent of the same sense-field, or, if it is one of the data by which the field is bounded, is indirectly related by r, in the manner I have explained, to some constituent of an " adjoining " field. And these structural properties of being asymmetrical, transitive and connected are assigned also to R, and to all the other higher order relations that are modelled on sense-given spatial relations, in the way that R is modelled on r. Consequently, one comes to hold that if any material thing X stands in any direction S from any other material thing Y, then Y does not stand in the direction S from X but in the converse direction ; that if X stands in the direction S from Y, and Y stands in the direction S from a third thing Z, then X stands in the direction S from Z ; and further, that there is always some material thing that stands in any given direction from any given material thing.[1] And I believe that this is all that is essentially involved in the ordinary conception of physical space.

It appears then, if my account of this matter is even substantially correct, that our conception of material things as having a continued and distinct existence in physical space, so far from involving any *a priori* intuition, can be derived from purely empirical and contingent features of our visual, tactual and kinaesthetic experiences.[2] I have found it convenient to deal with this problem as if it were a question of constructing one sort of objects out of

[1] Cf. Kaila, *op. cit.* pp. 44-9.

[2] With regard to physical space, this point is well brought out by Henri Poincaré in his " L'Espace et la Géométrie ", *La Science et l'Hypothèse*, ch. iv.

another ; but, strictly, it should be viewed as a problem about the reference of words. For what my construction of the physical world amounts to is a very general and simplified description of the main assumptions about the structure of phenomena that are involved in the everyday use of physical terms.

24. APPEARANCE AND REALITY

That the course of our sense-experience is not completely uniform is shown by the fact that the world of material things is found to be subject to change. But it is not always the case that a break in the uniformity of our sense-data is taken as a sign of an objective change in the material world. For we sometimes find that the perceptions to which the " discordant " sense-data give rise are qualitatively or existentially delusive ; we find that the sense-data endow material things with qualities that they do not really possess, or even that the material things that they seem to present do not exist at all. But how can one distinguish these cases from the others ? By what criteria does one determine whether or not a sense-datum presents a material thing as it really is ? We may dispose of the case of existentially delusive perceptions by referring to the foregoing analysis of the constitution of material things. For we may say that the occasions where a perception is held to be existentially delusive are those on which the form or the context of a sense-datum would lead one to assume that it belonged to a group of sense-data of the kind I have been describing, whereas, in fact, one's expectation of being able to sense further members of the group would not be capable of being fulfilled. But what of the perceptions that are held to be qualitatively delusive ? In this case, the sense-datum on which the perception is based does belong to a group which is constitutive of a material thing, but it is not an " honest " representative of the group, inasmuch as its presentation of the material thing is in some manner incorrect. If one is deceived by it, one will attribute to the thing some character that it does not really have. If one is not deceived one may say that the thing really has the character x, but that it appears to have the character y. Accordingly, the problem is to discover what differences among sense-data underlie this particular distinction between " appearance " and " reality ". And to answer this will be to furnish an explanation of the use of the word " real " as it is applied to the characteristics of material things.

It has already been made clear that the distinction between real and apparent characteristics does not enter into the domain of sense-data themselves.[1] Nor is there anything in a sense-datum, considered wholly by itself, by which one can decide whether or not it presents a material thing as it really is. Suppose that one has the experience of perceiving a round coin which looks elliptical, or that of perceiving a red flower which looks purple. One can describe

[1] *Vide* Part II.

these experiences by saying that one of them comprises the occurrence of a sense-datum which really is elliptical, and the other the occurrence of a sense-datum which really is purple. In neither case, however, does the relevant material thing really have the characteristic that the sense-datum makes it appear to have. But the reason for this cannot lie simply in the qualities of the sense-data ; for it may well be the case that sense-data with these qualities are not deceptive in this way at all. This particular coin, which looks elliptical, may really be round ; and this particular flower, which looks purple, may really be red ; but it is not impossible that a thing that looked elliptical should really be elliptical, or that one that looked purple should really be purple. And, conversely, in the cases where a sense-datum does present the real character of the material thing which is constituted by the group to which it belongs, it is always possible that on other occasions a sense-datum of the same quality may not be a faithful representative of its group. But if this distinction does not depend upon a difference in the intrinsic qualities of sense-data, it must depend upon a difference in their relations. And so we must try to discover what is the special relationship in which a sense-datum must stand to other sense-data, if it is to be accounted a bearer of the real character of the relevant material thing.

The first expedient that suggests itself is to look for our criterion in the nature of the context in which the sense-datum occurs. For one is inclined to think that the reason why a perception is qualitatively delusive is to be found in the accompanying conditions ; that a thing appears, for example, to have a different shape from that which it really has because it is seen from an abnormal angle, or that its colour is falsified because it is seen in an imperfect light. Accordingly, one might attempt to give a general description, in terms of sense-data, of what are conventionally taken to be preferential conditions ; and then one might say that the sense-data that were bearers of the real characters of the material things to which they belonged were those that occurred in conditions of this sort. Thus, the real shape of the material thing might be defined by a reference to the shape of sense-data that were in a certain spatial relationship to sense-data belonging to the observer's body ; or its real colour might be defined by a reference to sense-data that occurred in sense-fields displaying a relatively high degree of illumination, where the degree of illumination would be taken as a sensory characteristic of the field. But while this method may lead to correct results so far as it goes, it is not altogether satisfactory. One difficulty is that these preferential conditions are not the same for every kind of material thing. Thus, to take only one obvious example, the choice of an optimal distance from which to view an object depends to some extent upon the object's size. Let us assume, however, that the different cases can be classified in such a way that it is possible to specify the contexts that determine the selection of the correct sense-data out of any given group. Even so, there will remain the further objection that this process of selection is made to seem entirely arbitrary. Admittedly, the attribution of the characteristics of certain members of a group of sense-data to the material thing which is supposed to be constituted by the group as a whole is a matter of convention. But surely this convention serves some empirical purpose ? Must there not be some reason why the sense-data that occur in special sorts of contexts are given this preference over the other members of their groups ?

I think that there is a reason, and that it consists in the fact, which some philosophers have recognized,[1] that the privileged sense-data are found to be the most reliable members of the groups to which they belong, in the sense that they have the greatest value as sources of prediction. Thus, if I have obtained from my past experience a knowledge of the general feature of certain sequences of sense-data which may be described as the blurring of objects as their distance from the observer increases beyond a certain point, I am able from a near view of an object to infer how it will look from farther off ; but if I am seeing an object for the first time from a considerable distance, I am not able, by the use of any general laws of perspective, to infer with the same degree of accuracy how it will look from near at hand. Or again, if I am placed " too near " the object, I am not able, if I am seeing it for the

---

[1] *E.g.* Kaila, *op. cit.* pp. 22 -9, and Price, *op. cit.* p. 211.

first time to infer precisely what sense-data of it
will be presented if I go a little farther away ; but
if I start with the sense-data that are obtained from
this more remote position, together with a knowledge
of the manner of the blurring of appearances that
accompanies a decrease of distance from such a
point, I can more accurately calculate what sense-
data will be obtained if I approach the object more
nearly. And similar distinctions can be drawn among
the sense-data that belong to the other relevant types
of series, such as those that accompany variations in
the light. Thus, to take a negative example, the
use of dark glasses is held to be a distorting medium
in respect of colour, because the sense-data of colour
that occur under this condition have a minimal
predictive value ; for if one sees an object for the
first time through dark glasses, one cannot at all infer
what shade of colour it will appear when the glasses
are removed. The choice of the preferential conditions may not be the same for every kind of
material thing ; but it will be governed by the
general rule of giving preference to the sense-data
that are the most reliable, in the foregoing sense.
And so we come to conceive of these sense-data as
the " standard " members of their groups, from
which the others systematically deviate.[1] And it is

---

[1] Cf. Price, *op. cit.* pp. 209-15. But he is mistaken in supposing that " the fact that common sense is trying to state when it
says that x is the real quality of a material thing M " is merely
that the relevant qualities of the sense-data which belong to M
can be made to form a unity of system with x as its centre. For
this can be achieved even when x is not the real quality of the
material thing. Thus his criterion does not enable one to dis-

by reference to them that we determine the real, as opposed to the merely apparent, characteristics of the material thing which is constituted by the group in question. Generally speaking, the privileged sense-data in relation to colour are those that, in comparison with the other members of their groups, are the most conspicuously differentiated in this respect from the other constituents of their sense-fields ; in relation to shape, they are those that combine the greatest specific detail with the most clearly defined outline. And this means that their greater reliability is not evinced only in relation to other members of their groups. For they will also be the ones that are the least likely to betray us into the incorrect predictions which are involved in what is described as the mistaking of one material thing for another.

I have chosen my examples from the sense of sight because, as I have already pointed out, it is, for those who are able to obtain them, the visual data that play the predominant rôle in the construction of the material world. But the same principles govern our application of the distinction between appearance and reality to the physical qualities that are manifested to the other senses. Thus, if I wish to determine the real character of a person's voice, I do not take as my standard the sense-data that I obtain when I hear it over a defective telephone, or

tinguish between the case of a thing which is really round but sometimes looks elliptical, and that of a thing which is really elliptical but sometimes look round. His error is that he neglects to make any reference to the contexts in which the sense-data occur.

from a considerable distance; for they may have relatively small predictive values in comparison with certain other sense-data which, in virtue of their common association with a single visuo-tactual construct, are assigned to the same auditory group. And it is for a similar reason that if I wished to determine how a thing really tasted, I should not rely on the sense-data which I obtained when I had a severe cold; or that if my finger-tips were severely burned, I should not regard the tactual sense-data which I then obtained as indicative of the tactual consistency which really characterized the material thing in question. In none of these cases is it significant to say that the sense-data which occur in such abnormal conditions are themselves in any way illusory. But they may be judged to give a false impression of the material things with which they are associated, inasmuch as they fall short of the standard of reliability which is set by certain other members of their groups.

It is characteristic of the domain of tactual sense-data that while it is poorer in content than the visual domain, there is a sense in which it may be said to exhibit a greater measure of uniformity. For in the groups of tactual sense-data which help to constitute particular material things there tend to be fewer distortion series than in the groups which are their visual counterparts. And no doubt it is this that has led certain philosophers to identify the real characteristics of material things with those that are manifested to the sense of touch. But this is to overlook the fact that illusions of touch, though less common than illusions of sight, do nevertheless occur. And the refusal to make use of any visual data whatsoever in determining the real characteristics of material things is a plain departure from ordinary usage, and surely an unjustified impoverishment of our conception of the material world.

It is true, however, that this factor of sensible constancy, which is especially characteristic of tactual sense-data, is one to which we do attach very great importance. For it is this that leads to the introduction of a superior criterion of the reality of certain physical characteristics, the criterion of measurement. The use of the word " reality " which here comes into question is of a different order from that which I have so far been considering. For I have been concerned with the cases in which the determination of what is physically real consists in ascribing the sensible characteristics of certain privileged members of a group of sense-data to the group as a whole. But in the case where a numerically measurable value is given to what is held to be a real characteristic of a material thing, this characteristic is not manifested by any individual sense-datum of the group which constitutes the material thing in question. For the process of measurement is not a matter of discrimination within the group, but of correlating members of the group with those of another. Thus, in the case of a simple measurement of length, it is a matter of correlating visual or tactual sense-data which belong to the object that is being measured with visual or tactual sense-data which belong to the group that constitutes the measuring instrument. But even so the underlying principle that governs this use of the word " real " is the same as in the other case. For it is characteristic of the sensible relations from which such measurements are derived that they exhibit a very high degree of constancy.[1] The appearance of the thing that is measured and of the measuring instrument itself may vary to a considerable extent in different perceptual conditions, but the appearance of coincidence between them usually remains unaffected ; and it is upon this relation of coincidence that the measurement is based. If we add to this greater constancy the convenience of the mathematical terminology which they enable us to introduce, it becomes clear that the phenomena of measurement have a markedly high predictive value ; and it is for this reason that they are taken to furnish a superior criterion of the reality of the physical characteristics to which they apply. It is then by an extension of this principle that, when a technical scientific language is devised for describing the phenomena that enter into certain complicated processes of measurement, people are inclined to attribute an exclusive, or at any rate superior, reality to the scientific " objects " to which they suppose that the terms of such a language refer.[2] And here it may be noted that a similar reservation of the use of the word " real " for what can be quantitatively measured is to be found in the dis-

[1] Cf. Kaila, *op. cit.* pp. 64-8 and 82-6.   [2] Cf. pp. 221-2.

tinction which philosophers have made between primary and secondary qualities.[1] For what distinguishes the so-called ideas of primary qualities from the others is pre-eminently the part they can be made to play in processes of measurement. But it is not correct to go on to maintain, as some philosophers have done, that it is only the ideas of primary qualities that can have literal counterparts in the physical world. For, quite apart from the fallaciousness of the causal, or representative, theories of perception with which such a view is commonly associated, it is a mistake to suppose that because an apparent physical characteristic cannot be directly subjected to the criterion of measurement, it cannot properly be said to be " real " in any sense at all.

Finally, we must notice yet another use of the distinction between reality and illusion, in which these terms are understood to apply, not simply to the content of this or that perceptual judgement, but to whole segments of our perceptual histories. In this sense, a series of perceptions which satisfy the foregoing tests may still turn out to be delusive. I may find among my sense-data the relations that justify me in grouping them to form material things ; I may apply the authorized methods for assigning to these things their " real characteristics " ; I may even have such experiences as I should ordinarily describe by saying that I was making use of the criteria of measurement ; and still I may wake to find that I have been dreaming all along ; or I may

[1] Cf. pp. 33-5.

be persuaded by the testimony of other observers that the whole of this strand of my experience was a prolonged illusion, if I find that the hypothesis that this testimony itself is genuine fits in with my current experience. But this further, over-riding, distinction between appearance and reality does not bring in any new principle. For the only way in which one can test whether a series of perceptions is veridical, in this sense, is to see whether it is substantiated by further sense-experiences ; so that once again the ascription of " reality " depends upon the predictive value of the sense-data on which the perceptions are based. So long as the general structure of my sense-data conforms to the expectations that I derive from the memory of my past experience, I remain convinced that I am not living in a dream ; and the longer the series of successful predictions is extended, the smaller becomes the probability that I am mistaken. Admittedly, this progressive limitation of the probability of illusion can never reach the status of a formal demonstration. But then, as I have already [1] shown, it is unreasonable to expect that it should. The most that we can do is to elaborate a technique for predicting the course of our sensory experience, and to adhere to it so long as it is found to be reliable. And this is all that is essentially involved in our belief in the reality of the physical world.

[1] Part I, section 4.

INDEX

THE END

PRINTED BY R. & R. CLARK, LTD., EDINBURGH